T0368813

To my big, mad family:
my lifelong meal companions,
biggest champions and greatest loves

Tucking In

A Very Comforting Cookbook

Sophie
Wyburd

EBURY
PRESS

This is a book I have always wanted to write – an ode to feeding people. I have always been obsessed with eating. My favourite hobbies include asking what we are having for dinner whilst polishing off my breakfast, and plotting up plans for the next gathering around my table as soon as the dishes from the last one have been put away. Dreaming of food and eating has been a consistent thread throughout my life – the joy and intimacy that you extract from sitting around a table with old friends (and maybe handsome strangers too), quite literally breaking bread, is limitless, and just about my favourite activity ever.

I come from a big family, and much of the action growing up was centred around the dinner table. Every evening, my parents, my four sisters and I would gather around the table. Electronic devices were barred (even, for a brief spell, dramatically deposited in a glass bowl at the end of the table to be picked up later) and we would have a really good natter while tucking into something hearty. There was lots of chat, along with occasional slanging matches and physical fights, but mostly laughter. It was casual, but it was important, and it was formative.

Feeding people is my love language. As a child, when my parents had people over for dinner, I'd tiptoe out of my bedroom to peek through the bannisters and listen to the sounds of glasses clinking and people cackling. It was so damn glamorous! As a teenager, I craved the adultness of getting people around a table myself, and as soon as I could, I was hosting these kinds of meals. Whether it was an enormous vat of sausage ragu for a long table of friends as we left school, or the full Christmas spread tackled single-handedly in my breezeblock university halls, I took on the challenge with gusto – although, admittedly, not always with good results. You have to cook a few dodgy meals before you cook a good one. From all this, I figured out the way to feed people in the least stressful, and most enjoyable, way possible. When done right, cooking is a joy, and you can spread that joy by merrily feeding all your friends.

Feeding people is my love language.

Having people around for a bite to eat comes in many forms. It could be your dearest friend dropping over for a bowl of something warming on the sofa on a Tuesday night, or a crowd of ten squeezing around your garden table on mismatched chairs on a sunny Saturday afternoon. This book aims to make all acts of feeding people a non-stressful, casual affair. Cooking is often turned into a fussier thing than it needs to be – good food does not mean complicated food. Nobody wants to pop round to your house on a Wednesday for a fine-dining experience; they are there to chat and have a nice time. With this in mind, simplicity is at the heart of all the food that I cook, and the food that is in this book. It is not haute cuisine – it is hearty, comforting stuff packed with flavour; generous food with sharing at its core (generosity is key – I would be absolutely mortified if someone left my house hungry).

Passing around steaming bowls of food for people to dig into while having a natter is one of the greatest joys in life, and the cook should be revelling in that as much as anyone else around the table. Gone are the dinners of the past with plated starters, mains and puds, and a cook flailing around while a duck also flails around in an à l'orange sauce. You should not be chained to the stove while the laughter roars on next door. And you don't have to be! Keep it simple and doable, and you too can be the life and soul of the party, even if it is just an incredibly chill party of two.

There are lots of easy wins in this book. Many of these dishes feel super special, but most use pretty standard ingredients, and take very little effort or skill to throw together. For the adventurous cooks, there are some slightly more ambitious things you can whip up when you have more time and inclination, but I'm still not asking you to use any really mad kit or ingredients. Lots of these recipes can be made within 30 minutes, or prepped way in advance, to make the whole act of cooking as relaxed as can be. Many of them are intended as midweek meals – things you can quickly cook up in no time at all, but still feel exciting enough to feed to someone you love (and they will be left even more

enamoured with you than they were before). The majority of meals here can be eaten as a main, but also work nicely as part of a big feast, paired with a few more dishes. These recipes are often versions of things that I've cooked many, many times over the years, and I hope they will become equally trusty friends to you, to be whipped out of your back pocket whenever you need to feed people something delicious.

This book is a love letter to the people who have fed me, and all the people I have fed. My family and my friends are irrefutably the greatest things about my life, and you will find this book sprinkled with touches of them throughout. I hope that you get to cook these recipes for your loved ones too, and can keep the chain of feeding-people-as-a-love-language going. I find that cooking is not only a fabulous way to show other people that you love them; it's also a pretty foolproof method of showing yourself some love. There is nothing I find more soothing after a long day than tinkering away at the hob with the radio playing, stirring my worries away. If cooking and feeding make you feel all warm and fuzzy inside like they do me, or you are hoping to locate this feeling within yourself, I hope this book will become a firm friend of yours.

Sophie x

This book is a love letter to the people who have fed me, and all the people I have fed.

Cook's Notes
(a Sophie Wyburd glossary, if you will)

- I mostly encourage you to **season to taste**, rather than giving exact measurements, particularly when finishing a sauce or a dish in its entirety. This is for two reasons. Firstly, I am not a precise cook. I like feeling my way through a dish by tasting it often, and adjusting where needed, and rarely measure out things like salt at home. I would encourage you to do the same. Secondly, I am a salt fiend, and if I give you a precise measurement, and that is too much for your palate, then I may very well ruin your meal, and I don't want that. Add salt in small increments to get to a place where you feel comfortable. I will only give a salt measurement if it is for something that you cannot taste, e.g. raw meat or cake batter.

- When I talk about **salt**, I always mean flaky sea salt, except when I am using it to salt water to cook pasta or vegetables, or when baking cakes or bread. For these, use fine sea salt. Not to be confused with table salt, which I would never recommend using.

- When referring to an **egg**, I mean a large egg. Always buy free-range, and occasionally treat yourself to a Burford Brown or similarly golden-yolked thing when eating it as is, or when making homemade pasta.

- When I say **olive oil**, I mean extra virgin olive oil. Buy the best you can afford – it will lift your pastas and salads to dizzying heights. I have no qualms about sweating down veg in it. If it's good enough for the Italians, it's good enough for me.

- Always buy the best-quality **tomatoes** you can afford. Dodge the sad, pallid ones in bags, and go for bright red, plump guys on the vine.

- **Onions** come in all kinds of sizes, but I normally reach for one that is bang in the middle of the spectrum. Not the size of your head, or the size of a tangerine, but somewhere in between.

- When I say a small **bunch of herbs**, I mean one of those little bags you get in the supermarket, normally 25g. By all means, buy the chunkier bunches you get in greengrocers', but only use a handful of the herbs in this instance.

- **Kashmiri chilli powder** is always the type I reach for, owing to its bright red colour and mild flavour. I would encourage you to seek it out, but mild chilli powder will do in its place.

- I buy **salted butter**, as there is little I find more upsetting than getting a block of butter from the fridge and liberally spreading it on a crumpet to find that it tastes of nothing. To avoid this ever happening, you will never find unsalted butter in my fridge. Salt brings all flavours to life, and though unsalted butter is useful for some things (hollandaise, or some baked goods), nothing in this book requires it.

- I have marked lots of recipes as **gluten-free**, but would still recommend checking the packaging of ingredients before buying them if you are cooking for a gluten-free person. Many products such as stock cubes and sauces sneakily have it in there, so it is best to check.

- You'll find the following **dietary symbols** in the book, (Vg) for vegan recipes, (V) for vegetarian recipes, (P) for pescatarian recipes, (Df) for dairy-free recipes and (Gf) for gluten-free recipes.

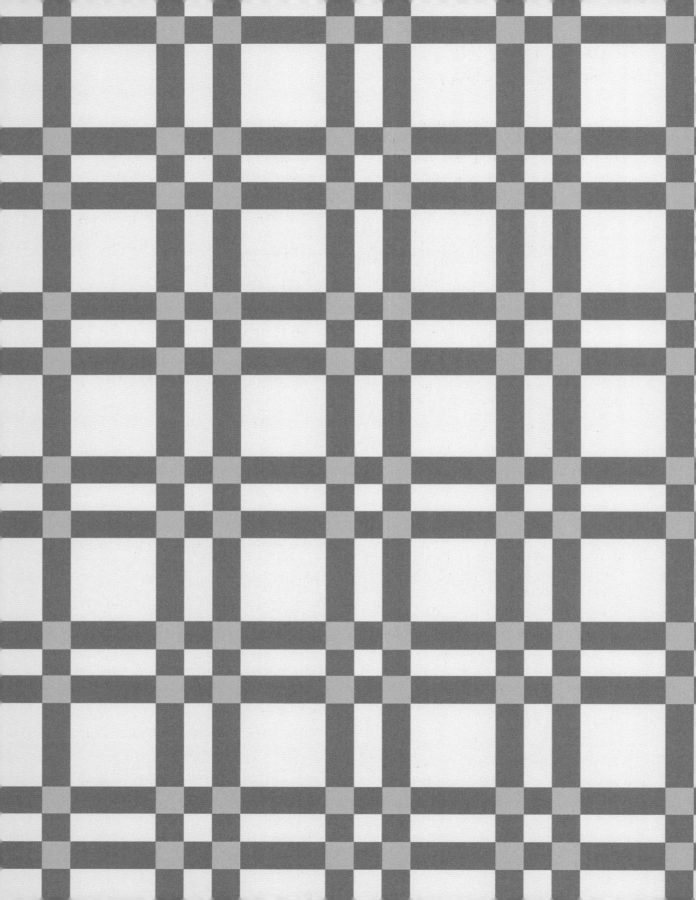

Nibbly Bits

I have always been the person who lurks near the kitchen when canapés (or can-apps) come out at a party. I struggle to hold a conversation if there is a risk of missing out. Although 'canapé' is a strong word for what you will find here, my love for nibbly things transfers to pretty much all settings. Lots of these recipes are for bits to bring out before the main event, but others would be grand at a picnic, or even as a snack in front of the telly. If people are coming to mine for a slap-up meal, they will never find a plated starter. They are far more likely to receive a few platters to graze on – dips, nibbles, or an array of bits I've bought and zhuzhed up in an aesthetically pleasing way. Some of the recipes in this chapter are more steppy, for those days when you are feeling extra. Others are hardly recipes at all.

Grazing Platters Three Ways

Serves
6–8

Prep time
15 minutes

Sometimes, you have arranged to get people around to yours, and you just cannot be bothered to cook anything, or perhaps you were so late leaving the office that you quite frankly don't have the time. This happens to all of us. On these occasions, it is totally acceptable to buy a bunch of things in the supermarket, and arrange them nicely on a plate. Your friends will be so blown away by your aesthetically pleasing display that they will not care that you didn't turn on the oven. This is the ultimate British spread of 'picky bits', and everyone loves picky bits. These three platters are not 'recipes', but guidelines for which bits I think work nicely together. Mix and match to your heart's content, of course.

The Classic Meat-and-Cheese Fest One

200g saucisson

200g Comté cheese

8 ripe figs

punnet of green grapes

jar of pickled chillies
(about 350g)

jar of cornichons
(about 340g)

1 really ripe soft cheese
(Époisses, Pié d'Angloys, or Langres would be great here)

1 baguette

100g butter

1   Slice your saucisson into little rounds, cut your Comté into 2mm triangular slices, and halve your figs. Using scissors, snip the grapes into little clusters. Drain your chillies and cornichons from their juices.

2   Get your chosen serving platter or board, and place your ripe soft cheese off-centre. Place your saucisson in a bowl and pop this on the opposite side. Slice the baguette into pieces, and place these in a serving bowl, or directly onto the board. Cluster your Comté slices on the board, as well as your grapes. Dot your figs, chillies and cornichons around the board to fill any gaps.

3   Serve up your grazing platter with lots of knives, with the butter and baguette on the side.

The Fresh Mediterranean One

6 baby cucumbers

punnet of red grapes

200g shop-bought tzatziki

2 tubs of mini ricotta-
or feta-stuffed peppers
(about 145g each)

jar of pitted kalamata olives
(about 290g)

jar of pitted fat green olives
(about 290g)

2 pots of stuffed vine leaves
(about 300g each)

165g herby pitta chips

salt and olive oil

1   Quarter the baby cucumbers lengthways. Using scissors, snip the grapes into little clusters.

2   Pour your tzatziki into a small serving bowl and drizzle it with 2 tablespoons of olive oil. Place this off-centre towards the middle of your serving platter or board, then arrange the cucumber in a cluster. Sprinkle the cucumber with a pinch of salt. Do a cluster of grapes, followed by your stuffed peppers, olives, stuffed vine leaves and pitta chips, making sure you are plugging any gaps in the board with ingredients.

3   Serve up your grazing board with some napkins.

The One With All the Veg

300g baby heritage carrots

2 red endives

400g radishes

250g cherry tomatoes
on the vine

2 tubs of grilled artichoke
hearts *(about 140g each)*

2 x 150g packs of garlic
and herb cream cheese
(I like Boursin)

100g smoked almonds

90g sourdough crackers
(I like the Peter's Yard ones)

140g olive grissini

1   Scrub any tough bits on the outsides of your carrots with a clean scourer. I prefer doing this to peeling them, as you waste less and the carrots keep their shape. Halve the carrots lengthways. Chop the ends off your endives to separate the leaves, trimming off a bit extra when you need to in order to release the next layer. Halve your radishes. Using scissors, snip the cherry tomato vines into little clusters. Drain the artichoke hearts.

2   Unwrap the cheeses and place them off-centre, at opposite ends of your serving platter or board. Arrange your carrots in a cluster on the board, then go in with your endives, radishes, cherry tomatoes, artichoke hearts, smoked almonds and crackers, making sure you plug any gaps with the ingredients.

3   Place your grissini in a tall glass. Serve up the grazing board with the grissini on the side.

Farinata with Datterini and Pine Nut Salsa

Serves
8

Cook time
1 hour, plus resting

150g gram flour

2 rosemary sprigs

For the salsa
2 onions

30g pine nuts

½ small bunch of parsley

100g semi-dried datterini tomatoes

salt, pepper and olive oil

Pictured on page 16

Tip

This farinata makes brilliant nibbles when cut into squares, but could also be a light meal in and of itself, served with a crisp salad.

Purists will say that farinata should be eaten hot from the oven, and by itself, without toppings. While I agree that it must be eaten hot, and it is incredibly lovely solo, as a nibble I do think it benefits from a colourful garnish. Here, north Italian farinata meets a southern Italian-style topping in the form of caramelised onions, pine nuts and sun-dried tomatoes. I have always found sun-dried tomatoes to be pretty naff, maybe due to their prevalence in the 90s alongside a prosciutto-wrapped chicken breast and balsamic glaze. However, Odysea make some gorgeous semi-dried datterini ones that have changed the game with their juiciness.

1 Sift the gram flour into a large mixing bowl. Make a well in the middle, then add 300ml water and 3 tablespoons of olive oil. Whisk until smooth, only whisking in one direction to ensure that it gets smooth. Cover the top of your bowl with cling film or paper towels, and leave to sit at room temperature for at least 2 hours.

2 Meanwhile, make the salsa. Peel, halve and finely slice your onions. Heat 6 tablespoons of olive oil in a small saucepan over a very low heat, then tip in the onions, along with a pinch of salt. Cook for 25 minutes until they are totally soft. Add occasional splashes of water if the onions look like they are sticking to the pan.

3 Toast the pine nuts in a frying pan over a medium heat for 3 minutes, until lightly browned. Remove from the pan and allow to cool slightly.

4 Finely chop your parsley, and drain the semi-dried datterini tomatoes from their oil.

5 Returning to your onions, increase the heat to medium-high, and cook them for another 10 minutes until they are really caramelised, stirring frequently to ensure that they don't stick and burn. Add the semi-dried tomatoes, along with the pine nuts and parsley. Stir to combine, then season to taste with salt.

6 Preheat your oven to 270°C/250°C fan/gas mark 10, or as hot as it will go.

7 Pick the rosemary leaves, then add these to the batter along with 1 teaspoon of salt. Give it a whisk.

8 Line a baking dish (about 30 x 22cm) with parchment, add 4 tablespoons of olive oil, then pour in your batter. Place in the oven and bake for 10 minutes until the farinata is sizzling. It should be crispy and golden around the edges, with a set yellow middle.

9 Let it cool slightly to set further, then cut it into 4cm squares. Top each square with a little salsa, then serve while they are still warm.

Dressed-Up Hummus Three Ways

Nobody is above buying supermarket dips. In fact, you should embrace the ease of them. To make them feel more exciting, I almost always decant them into a pretty little bowl, and top them with something lovely to swirl a crisp through. Sometimes, that is just a lick of olive oil and some toasted seeds, but other times I like to make it a fancier affair. Hummus is for every occasion: I'd bring it to a potluck; I'd eat it around the garden table; I may very well even eat it in the bath. Here are three of my favourite ways to make shop-bought hummus slightly more interesting.

Curry Leaf Tarka

Cook time
10 minutes

4 garlic cloves

½ small bunch of fresh curry leaves

1 tsp cumin seeds

1 tbsp nigella seeds

½ tsp kashmiri chilli powder
(or mild chilli powder)

½ tsp ground turmeric

200g tub of hummus

salt and rapeseed oil

Pictured on page 16

1 Peel and finely slice your garlic cloves.

2 Pour 6 tablespoons of rapeseed oil into a small frying pan. Tip in your sliced garlic, then place the pan over a medium heat. This will stop the garlic burning and bring it up to a crisp gradually.

3 Once your garlic has sizzled for about a minute, tip in your curry leaves and cumin seeds. Let these all pop for a minute, then remove the pan from the heat just as the garlic starts to turn golden. Tip in your nigella seeds, chilli powder and turmeric.

4 Spoon the hummus into your chosen serving bowl and swoosh it around a bit. Spoon over your curried oil, then add a little sprinkle of salt. Serve with your favourite dippy bits.

Chipotle Onion and Chickpea

Cook time
45 minutes

1 onion

½ tsp cumin seeds

400g tin of chickpeas

1 tsp sweet smoked paprika

1 tbsp chipotle paste

200g tub of hummus

salt and olive oil

1 Preheat your oven to 220°C/200°C fan/gas mark 7.

2 Peel, halve and finely slice your onion. Heat 4 tablespoons of olive oil in a small saucepan over a medium heat, then tip in the cumin seeds and onion. Add a pinch of salt, then cook for 30 minutes until the onion is very soft. Add occasional splashes of water intermittently – you want the onion to be really deeply caramelised, but the water will stop it catching too much on the base of the pan.

3 While the onions cook, drain the chickpeas in a colander, then pat them dry with some paper towels. Tip them into a baking tray, then drizzle over 2 tablespoons of olive oil, and sprinkle over the smoked paprika and ½ teaspoon of salt. Give them a good toss so that the chickpeas are all totally coated, then bake them for 25 minutes until they are super crispy.

4 Returning to your onions, turn up the heat to high, and cook for another 5–10 minutes until they are really caramelised. Add the chipotle paste, and give it all a good mix. Season to taste with salt.

5 Spoon your hummus into a serving bowl and swoosh it around. Top with your spicy onions and a good sprinkling of crispy chickpeas. Serve it up with your favourite crisps and dips.

Walnut Dukkah

Cook time
20 minutes

50g walnuts

1 tbsp coriander seeds

1 tbsp fennel seeds

1 tsp cumin seeds

2 tbsp sesame seeds

1 tsp dried oregano

200g tub of hummus

salt, pepper and olive oil

1 Preheat your oven to 200°C/180°C fan/gas mark 6.

2 Tip your walnuts into a small baking tray, along with the coriander seeds, fennel seeds, cumin seeds and sesame seeds. Bake in the oven for 8 minutes until they are fragrant and toasted.

3 Pour your nut, seed and spice mix into a pestle and mortar, then pound it to a fine crumb. Add your dried oregano to the mix, along with 15 twists of black pepper. Season to taste with salt, then give it a good mix. This is your dukkah.

4 Spoon your hummus into a serving bowl and swoosh it around. Drizzle over 2 tablespoons of olive oil, then sprinkle over a good handful of the dukkah. You won't use all the dukkah in this recipe, but it will keep for a few weeks in an airtight tin, and tastes good sprinkled on pretty much anything – try it with eggs, salads and grilled meats.

Candied Chilli and Pistachio Whipped Ricotta

Serves

6

Cook time

20 minutes, plus soaking

50g pistachio kernels

120g green chillies

3 garlic cloves

50g caster sugar

50ml white wine vinegar

1 tsp cumin seeds

250g ricotta

juice of ½ lemon

a big bag of your favourite crisps

salt, pepper and olive oil

Pictured on page 17

Dips are the new starters. More often than not, if people are round, I pop them down with a dip, and crunchy things to dunk into it, while I finish off the main bit of the meal. The dip will ordinarily be one of two things: a supermarket dip that I have zhuzhed up (see Dressed-Up Hummus on page 18), or a whipped ricotta number. Whipped ricotta dips are great because they look and sound a lot fancier than they are. The candied green chillies are the only real effort here, but even they are done in less than 20 minutes. All the elements can be prepped a day in advance, so you can spend more time curating the vibes and the good times, then assemble the dip when you are ready.

1 Boil your kettle. Put your pistachios into a heatproof bowl, then pour over enough boiling water to cover them. Leave them to sit for 30 minutes – this will soften them slightly.

2 To make your candied green chillies, finely chop the green chillies, seeds and all, either by hand or by pulsing them in a small food processor. Peel and finely chop your garlic, too.

3 Tip the caster sugar into a small saucepan, along with the vinegar and cumin seeds. Heat over a medium heat until the sugar has melted and dissolved. Add the green chillies and garlic, along with ½ teaspoon of salt, then simmer for 8–10 minutes until the mixture has thickened. Set aside to cool.

4 Move on to your whipped ricotta. Drain your pistachios, then place them in a clean tea towel, and wrap them up in a parcel. Rub to remove the brown skins and reveal the bright green nuts beneath, then pour them into a food processor. Whizz to break them up into a fine powder, then add the ricotta and lemon juice, along with 2 tablespoons of olive oil. Whizz it up until you have a smooth, light green paste. Season this to taste with salt.

5 Spoon your pistachio ricotta into a bowl, then top it with the candied green chillies (you will have about half left, which will keep in the fridge for a week and are delicious scattered over any meal you'd like to spice up). Drizzle on some more olive oil, then serve with your favourite bag of crisps for dipping – I personally love a salted crinkle-cut crisp.

Puttanesca Gildas

Makes

16

Prep time

5 minutes

16 pickled guindilla chillies

16 pitted kalamata olives

16 anchovies packed in oil

16 small sun-dried tomatoes

You will need 16 cocktail sticks

Pictured on page 17

Gildas are the ultimate classy beer snack. What's not to love about lots of salty, tinned things having a party on a skewer? The classic Basque versions, which I first ate in San Sebastian, involve a plump green olive, a chunk of pickled chilli and an anchovy, but I wanted to do a little twist on that by incorporating the flavours of everyone's favourite store-cupboard pasta dish – puttanesca! It legitimately takes more time to wash the oil off your hands than it does to assemble these, making them a perfect picky bit to land on when you are time-poor, but sense of taste-rich.

1   Halve the pickled chillies.

2   Get a cocktail stick, and use it to skewer an olive. Next skewer your anchovy a couple of times by folding it over itself on the cocktail stick. Add 2 pieces of pickled chilli, and a sun-dried tomato. Repeat these steps with your remaining skewers. Serve them up.

Green Olive Baked Camembert

Serves
6

Cook time
40 minutes

250g Camembert

60g pitted green olives

1 green chilli

½ small bunch of parsley

juice of ½ lemon

2 tbsp honey

grissini, *to serve*

salt and olive oil

Growing up in the early 2000s, there are a few foods I remember encountering for the first time that blew my tiny mind to smithereens. Baked Camembert is one of them. My mum's friend used to bake them in a sea of sweet chilli sauce and serve them topped with toasted walnuts; upon trying this, my eyes basically popped out like those of a very loved-up cartoon character. Baked Camembert may be considered a bit basic these days, but in honour of nine-year-old Sophie, I am including this recipe, of which I am very fond. Sharp, spicy olive salsa is an ideal thing to cut through the oozy, cheesy richness. I still think it is a phenomenal crowd-pleaser to bring out as part of a larger nibbly spread, or as a starter. In fact, this wouldn't go amiss on a grazing platter like the ones on pages 12–15.

1   Preheat your oven to 220°C/200°C fan/gas mark 7.

2   Remove the Camembert from its box and remove any plastic wrapping. Slot one of the box halves inside the other, then nestle your Camembert back inside. I find this reduces the chance of leakage. Place this on a baking tray, then bake for 25 minutes.

3   Meanwhile, very finely chop your olives, chilli and parsley.

4   Add the olives to a pestle and mortar, then bash them to a fine paste. Add the chilli and bash again, before adding the parsley, and doing the same. Drizzle in 3 tablespoons of olive oil, then finish with the lemon juice. Season this mixture to taste with salt.

5   Once your Camembert is cooked, drizzle it with your olive salsa and the honey. Serve with grissini for dunking, using them to swirl it all together.

Endive Cups with Goat's Cheese and Pickled Walnuts

Makes
about 30

Prep time
10 minutes

2 red endives

2 pickled walnuts

125g soft goat's cheese

2 tbsp honey

5 thyme sprigs

It took me a while to learn to love the bitter notes of red endive, but the second I did, we embarked on a pretty serious love affair. It is one of those vegetables that's so damn pretty that you hardly have to do anything to it at all. This is one of my favourite ways to eat it: smeared with some tangy goat's cheese and adorned with pickled walnuts, ready to be the chicest nibble at any party. It literally takes minutes to chuck together, and makes you look like quite the fancy pants.

1 Cut the end off your endives, and separate out the leaves. You may occasionally need to trim the ends again to release the next layer of leaves.

2 Cut your walnuts into rounds about 3mm thick.

3 Smear the cut end of each of your endive leaves with your soft goat's cheese. Place a piece of pickled walnut on top of each bit of goat's cheese, and arrange your endive cups on a serving platter. Drizzle over the honey, then pick the leaves off the thyme and sprinkle them over. Serve.

Corn Pakoras

Makes
12

Cook time
40 minutes

1 large onion

50g fresh spinach

1 red chilli

1 small floury potato
(about 170g)

195g tin of sweetcorn

150g gram flour

1 tbsp cumin seeds

1 tsp garam masala

3 tbsp tomato ketchup,
plus more to serve (check the
label if making gluten-free)

2 litres vegetable oil,
for frying

salt

Tip
These are best piping hot
from the pan, but are also very
enjoyable cold the next day.

I am thrilled to announce that I have been given the keys to the castle in the form of my partner Cam's family pakora recipe. I called his cousin Anita to get all the top tips, and discover what makes the Kumar pakora, pioneered by her mum Raj, so damn good. The secret ingredient? Ketchup. It gives tang to the batter, and also darkens the colour. In the absence of Raj's top-secret tamarind chutney, be sure to serve these up with a big puddle of ketchup for dipping, too. In typical family-recipe fashion, I was not given strict quantities, but guidelines. Anita says that the thinner the batter, the crispier the pakora, so I've very much gone for this vibe. You also want to make the batter just before you are ready to cook, as it will get too wet if it sits too long. The Kumars don't add corn to their pakoras, but I love the sweet little pops you get from it. Thank you Anita (and Raj) for all the help.

1   Peel, halve and finely slice the onion. Finely slice the spinach and red chilli, too. Peel and dice the potato into little 1cm cubes. It is important that they are cut small so that they cook through. Drain the sweetcorn.

2   Add all your veg to a large bowl, along with the gram flour, cumin seeds and garam masala. Give it a mix so that the gram flour is coating all the vegetables.

3   Pour in 190ml water, then add 1½ teaspoons of salt and the ketchup. Give it a mix so that it is all combined.

4   Pour your oil into a large saucepan so that it comes about a third of the way up the sides of the pan. Heat it over a medium heat so that it gently comes up to about 170°C. If you don't have a thermometer, carefully drop a little batter into the pan. If it sizzles, your oil is hot enough to begin cooking. If it browns too quickly, turn down the heat a little.

5   Take a small handful of the mixture loosely in your hand, and gently lower it into your oil pan, being careful not to touch the oil and burn your fingers. Add a couple more handfuls to the pan, then fry for about 5–7 minutes, turning them occasionally so that they brown evenly. You want them to be a deep nutty brown colour, and very crispy.

6   Lift the pakoras out of the pan with a slotted spoon, and drain them on a plate lined with paper towels. Keep them warm while you fry the rest.

7   Pile them all onto a plate, then serve with a big puddle of ketchup.

Smoked Trout and Pickle Pumpernickel Toasts

Makes
24

Cook time
30 minutes

3 slices of pumpernickel bread

small bunch of dill

2 spring onions

30g cornichons

50g capers

165g full-fat cream cheese

zest and juice of ½ lemon,
plus wedges to serve

100g smoked trout

salt, pepper and olive oil

This is a nibbly bit that I have insisted on making around Christmas time for a good few years now. Smoked salmon is a festive classic, but these days I'm leaning more towards her cousin, smoked trout, for my nibbles. Not only is she pinker, milder and less fatty, she is also a more sustainable fish option. I like the Scandinavian way of treating cured fish the best, with lots of pickled bits to cut through the richness, and dark rye as the vessel, so I've decided to lean that way in this recipe. The pickle-packed cream cheese mixture is so lovely that I sometimes make it just to smear on bagels. Highly recommend.

1 Preheat your oven to 190°C/170°C fan/gas mark 5.

2 Cut your pumpernickel bread into roughly 5cm squares. Arrange these on a large baking tray, and bake for 15 minutes until they have crisped up a little. Set aside to cool.

3 Meanwhile, make your pickle topping. Finely chop three-quarters of the dill, and slice the spring onions, green parts and all. Finely dice the cornichons, and chop 25g of the capers, too.

4 Tip all this chopped goodness into a medium-sized bowl, then add your cream cheese, along with the lemon zest and juice. Give it all a good mix, then season generously with salt and pepper.

5 Heat 2 tablespoons of olive oil in a small frying pan over a medium heat. Pat dry the remaining 25g of capers with paper towels, then tip them into the pan. Fry for 5 minutes until crispy. Lift them out of the pan with a slotted spoon, and leave to cool on a plate lined with paper towels.

6 Pick the remaining dill leaves off their stems.

7 Once your rye bread toasts have cooled, generously smear each one with cream cheese topping. Tear off pieces of smoked trout and place these on top, then scatter over your crispy capers and picked dill leaves. Serve with lemon wedges for squeezing.

Bloody Mary Prawn Cocktail Cups

Makes
20

Cook time
25 minutes

25g butter

2 tbsp tomato purée

50ml vodka

2 baby gem lettuces

small bunch of chives

100g mayonnaise

1 tsp Worcestershire sauce

a few drops of hot sauce
(I use Tabasco here)

juice of ½ lemon

300g peeled cold-water prawns

salt and pepper

Pictured on page 28

This Bloody Mary prawn trick is one I learned from Ben Lippett and Hannah Miller, while they were making some particularly gorgeous prawn rolls one day at the Mob office. Cooking tomato purée in brown butter gives you a really intense, nutty savouriness – one that packs a real punch in a mayonnaise. The additions of Worcestershire sauce and hot sauce make it quite Bloody Mary-esque, which is a nice little twist on a classic Marie Rose sauce. I think that a good old-fashioned tiny pink prawn is perfect here – the less fancy, the better. We are going for old-school prawn cocktail vibes, because who doesn't love that?

1 Melt your butter in a small saucepan over a medium-low heat. Let it brown; it will foam, and the little flecks of white in it will turn a caramel colour. Your kitchen will smell like biscuits.

2 Once this happens, add your tomato purée. Cook for about 5 minutes until it's nice and dark, and sticking to the base of the pan a bit. Add your vodka to deglaze the pan a little, and let it entirely reduce down. Remove the pan from the heat.

3 Cut the ends off your baby gem to separate the leaves. Finely chop your chives.

4 Add the mayonnaise to a bowl, along with your tomato purée mixture, the Worcestershire sauce and as much hot sauce as you can handle. Squeeze in the lemon juice and give it all a good mix.

5 Tip in the prawns, and give it a mix so that they are totally coated in the sauce, then adjust the seasoning with salt and pepper if needed.

6 Spoon a heaped tablespoon of the prawn mixture into each of your lettuce cups, then sprinkle the top with chives. Arrange on a plate, and serve.

Cheeseboard Arancini

Makes
36

Cook time
2 hours, plus chilling

1 large onion

2 garlic cloves

30g butter

a few fresh sage leaves

1.3 litres vegetable or
chicken stock

350g arborio risotto rice

150ml white wine

250g mixed cheese *(I use half
Stilton and half Cheddar, but any
combination of strong cheeses
from your cheeseboard will do)*

2 × 125g mozzarella balls

100g plain flour

3 eggs

180g panko breadcrumbs

2 litres vegetable oil, *for frying*

120g cranberry sauce

salt, pepper and olive oil

Pictured on page 28

While I was at university, I became obsessed with cooking arancini. I discovered that risotto was a perfect cheap meal, one I could rustle up from any strange vegetable lurking in the fridge, and making arancini was a way to make that meal go even further, very luxuriously. These arancini are intended to be served up as a nibble in the festive season, when you have a tonne of cheese kicking around in the fridge, and fancy a gooey, crispy place to put it. This recipe makes a load, but they freeze really well once breadcrumbed, so you could batch-cook and save some for comfort-food emergencies.

1   Peel, halve and finely dice your onion. Peel and finely chop your garlic cloves.

2   Heat the butter with 2 tablespoons of olive oil in a large sauté pan over a medium-low heat. Add the sage leaves and onion, and cook this mixture gently for 20 minutes until the onion has softened but hasn't taken on any colour. Add the garlic, then cook this out for 2 minutes.

3   Meanwhile, heat your stock in a small saucepan, and keep it warm over a low heat.

4   Add the risotto rice to the pan with the onion and lightly toast it in the butter for a few minutes until the grains start to turn translucent. Add the white wine and give the mixture a stir.

5   Once your rice has absorbed the wine, gradually add your stock in small increments. Stir all the while to allow your rice grains to absorb the stock before adding more liquid. It should take about 25 minutes for all your stock to be added and for your rice to become tender.

6   Grate your grate-able hard cheeses, and crumble the soft ones. Add the cheese to your risotto and give it a mix, then season to taste with salt and 20 twists of black pepper. The cheese will be pretty salty, so you won't need much.

7   Pour your risotto into a shallow dish and leave to cool. Cover the top with cling film, then pop into the fridge to chill for a few hours.

continues overleaf

Cheeseboard Arancini

8 Meanwhile, cut the mozzarella into 2cm cubes.

9 Once your risotto feels firm to touch, tip the flour into one bowl, whisk the eggs in another, and tip the breadcrumbs into a third. Season the flour with ½ teaspoon of salt.

10 Roll your risotto mixture into about 36 ping-pong-sized balls, each about 30g. Make a hollow in the middle of each one, then insert a piece of mozzarella. Seal the gap by pushing risotto into it and rolling the ball together with your hands again.

11 Dip the risotto balls in the flour, then the eggs, then the breadcrumbs, turning to coat, then set aside on a large baking tray lined with baking parchment. You could freeze them at this point.

12 Pour your vegetable oil into a large saucepan so that it comes about a third of the way up the sides of the pan. Heat it over a medium heat so that it gently comes up to about 180°C. If you don't have a thermometer, carefully sprinkle some breadcrumbs into the pan. If they sizzle, your oil is hot enough to begin cooking. If they brown quickly, turn down the heat a little. Once it is ready, carefully add your arancini, a few at a time, and fry for 5 minutes until crisp and golden. Remove with a slotted spoon, transfer to a plate lined with paper towels and keep warm while you repeat with your remaining arancini.

13 Serve with some cranberry sauce for dipping.

Mushroom Parfait Toasts

Makes

30

Cook time

1 hour, plus pickling and setting

5 slices of sourdough bread

a few sprigs of thyme

For the pickles

1 cucumber

250ml white wine vinegar

25g caster sugar

½ tsp mustard seeds

For the pâté

2 banana shallots

a few thyme sprigs

90g butter

50ml brandy

100ml red wine

600g chestnut mushrooms

75ml mirin

3 tbsp light soy sauce

salt, pepper and olive oil

Tip

You can make the pickles up to 2 weeks in advance and store in a sterilised container. The pâté can be made up to 3 days in advance.

Mushroom pâté is one of those dishes that gets foisted on vegetarians regularly, and often against their will. I was intent on developing a recipe for one that was legitimately delicious, and something you would not only gladly eat, but actively seek out. Fallow is a restaurant in London that does the silkiest mushroom pâté, which manages to feel incredibly meaty despite containing only vegetal things. It inspired me to try to make a similarly savoury affair at home. I like to swoosh this on squares of toast with a topping of pickled cucumber to make a blooming gorgeous canapé, but you can also simply serve it up with a pile of toast and pickles as a sharing plate. The world is your oyster!

1 First, make your pickles. Begin by finely slicing the cucumber into 2mm thick rounds.

2 Pour your white wine vinegar into a medium-sized saucepan, along with the sugar, mustard seeds, 1 teaspoon of salt and 250ml water. Place over a medium heat and bring to a gentle simmer, stirring it occasionally to dissolve the sugar.

3 Remove the pan from the heat, then add your cucumber slices to the pan. Let it cool to room temperature, then pour the whole mixture into a sealable container. Leave the cucumber to pickle in the fridge at least overnight, or for up to several weeks.

4 To make your pâté, peel, halve and finely slice the shallots. Add them to a small saucepan with the thyme and 20g of the butter, and cook down on a very low heat until the shallots have softened – this will take about 15 minutes.

5 Add your brandy and red wine to the pan. Increase the heat to medium, then cook for 15 minutes so that the liquid totally reduces to create a jammy onion mixture.

6 Finely slice the mushrooms. Heat your largest frying pan over a high heat, and add 1 tablespoon of olive oil. Add a third of your mushrooms to the pan and reduce the heat to medium-high. Fry for 5 minutes until the mushrooms are golden brown but not too dry. Tip them into a bowl, and repeat with the remaining mushrooms.

continues overleaf

Mushroom Parfait Toasts

7 Return all the mushrooms to the frying pan, then pour in your mirin and soy. Cook for about 2 minutes until the mushrooms have absorbed most of the liquid and are coated in a dark, glossy sauce.

8 Tip all the mushrooms into a blender, along with your shallot mixture. Melt the remaining butter in a small saucepan or microwave, then pour this into the blender too. Whizz up your mixture into a smooth paste, then season to taste with salt and pepper – the soy will have added a good amount of salt, but it may need a little more.

9 Spoon your pâté into a serving dish, then closely cover the surface with cling film. Pop it in the fridge to set for at least 2 hours.

10 When you're ready to serve, toast your bread slices in the toaster. Spread them with a thick coating of your pâté. Cut each piece of toast into 6 evenly sized rectangles or squares, top with your pickles and picked thyme leaves, then pop on a plate to serve. Alternatively, serve the pâté in a bowl, with a stack of toast and pickles on the side, for people to serve themselves.

Spiced Potato Rolls

Makes
16

Cook time
1 hour 30 minutes

500g Maris Piper potatoes

1 onion

1 tsp cumin seeds

½ tsp black mustard seeds

4 garlic cloves

2cm knob of ginger

1 green chilli

1 tsp ground turmeric

½ tsp kashmiri chilli powder
(or mild chilli powder)

1 tsp garam masala

100g frozen peas

2 tbsp lime pickle

50ml coconut oil

50ml maple syrup

500g puff pastry sheet

salt, pepper and vegetable oil

I first made these quite by accident when I had some leftover samosa filling kicking around in the fridge. I rolled it up in puff pastry to make a vegan sausage roll situation to take to a picnic, and found that the ones I made containing actual sausage were almost entirely neglected in favour of these. They are now a staple for summer picky bits, and it's no wonder when you consider this filling: spiced potato, bright lil peas and the punch of lime pickle make a glorious combo. I am very much an advocate of double carbs, and they are out in full force with this one. I was thrilled to learn that lots of shop-bought puff pastry is vegan-friendly – just make sure you double-check the label.

1   Peel and dice your potatoes into 1cm chunks. Tip them into a medium-sized saucepan filled with cold water and season to taste with salt. Bring to the boil, then simmer for 10 minutes, or until the potatoes are just tender. Drain in a colander and leave to steam dry.

2   While your potatoes cook, peel, halve and dice your onion.

3   Heat 3 tablespoons of vegetable oil in a sauté pan over a medium heat. Add your cumin seeds and mustard seeds, then cook out for a minute until fragrant and starting to pop.

4   Add the onion to the pan and cook for 15 minutes until soft and caramelised. Peel and finely chop your garlic and ginger, and finely dice your chilli. Add these to the pan and cook for another 2 minutes.

5   Add ½ teaspoon of the turmeric, along with the chilli powder and garam masala. Tip in the peas and cook for 5 minutes, then add the drained potatoes, followed by the lime pickle, stirring so that the potato chunks are totally coated in the spices and onions, and are breaking down at the edges ever so slightly. Season with 1 teaspoon of salt, then add 2 tablespoons of water and give it a mix. Set the mixture aside to cool.

6   Heat your coconut oil in the microwave for 30 seconds, or until it is liquid. Stir in the maple syrup and remaining turmeric. Unravel your puff pastry, then cut it in half lengthways.

continues overleaf

Spiced Potato Rolls

7   Place half the filling on each piece of pastry, arranging it in a line running down the length of each piece, slightly off-centre. Brush the other sides with your coconut oil mixture, then fold the cut sides over the potato in the middle to meet the opposite pastry edge. Press the edges down with a fork to seal, then brush the outside all over with more coconut oil. Cut each roll in half, then place on a baking tray and chill in the fridge for 20 minutes.

8   Preheat your oven to 220°C/200°C fan/gas mark 7.

9   Cut each of your 4 rolls into 4 pieces, giving you 16 in total, then lightly score diagonal incisions on the top of each. Place them, spaced well apart, on a large baking sheet lined with baking parchment. Bake for 15–20 minutes, or until the pastry is tender and golden.

10 Eat them hot from the oven, or allow them to cool entirely, and box up in sealable containers to take to a picnic. These will keep for 2 days in the fridge, sealed in an airtight container.

Sticky Sprunion Sausage Rolls

Makes
16

Cook time
1 hour

4 spring onions

2 garlic cloves

400g good-quality pork sausages

2 tbsp oyster sauce

1 tbsp dark soy sauce

1 tsp Chinese five-spice

½ tsp ground white pepper

500g puff pastry sheet

1 egg, beaten

2 tbsp sesame seeds

salt

Pictured on page 36

I cannot relate to people who don't like pastry. What's not to love about it? Crisp, fatty and flaky, I find it improves most things it touches. Sausages are a near-perfect food in my mind, but wrapping them in puff pastry propels them to the dizziest heights of excellence. I've made sausage rolls flavoured a bajillion ways – with cheese and Marmite, with mustard and herbs, with a fish sauce-rich curry paste – but this is a new favourite. Oyster sauce felt like a natural thing to stick in the mix to get the pork all sweet and sticky, and there's a tingle of five-spice running through it, along with lots of sprunions (spring onions). It's pretty outrageous to turn up to a picnic without a sausage roll, in my opinion, so you should probably consider cooking these for the next one you have to attend.

1   Finely slice your spring onions, green parts and all. Peel and finely chop your garlic.

2   Squeeze the sausage meat into a mixing bowl, discarding the skins. Add the spring onions to the bowl, along with the garlic, oyster sauce, soy sauce, five-spice, white pepper and ½ teaspoon of salt. Give it all a good mix.

3   Unravel your puff pastry, then cut it in half lengthways.

4   Place half the filling on each piece of pastry, arranging it in a line running down the length of each piece, slightly off-centre. Brush the sides with beaten egg, then fold the longer side over to meet the opposite edge. Press the edges down to seal, then brush the entire outside with more egg. Sprinkle the tops with sesame seeds, then cut each roll in half. Place them on a baking tray and chill in the fridge for 20 minutes.

5   Preheat your oven to 220°C/200°C fan/gas mark 7.

6   Cut each of your 4 rolls into 4 slices, giving you 16 in total, then place them, spaced well apart, on a large baking sheet. Cook for 15–20 minutes, or until the pastry is tender and golden.

7   Eat the sausage rolls while they are still hot, or allow them to cool completely and eat them cold. These will keep for 2 days in the fridge, sealed in an airtight container.

Tip

You can freeze these in an airtight container once they are cut into rolls, then bake them from frozen. Just add an extra 5 minutes to the cooking time.

Crispy Artichokes with Feta and Olive Dip

Serves
8–10

Cook time
30 minutes

200g feta

100g thick natural yoghurt

½ small bunch of dill

100g pitted kalamata olives

2 × 280g jars of artichoke hearts

2 litres vegetable oil, *for frying*

100g plain flour

40g cornflour

½ tsp baking powder

150ml fridge-cold sparkling water

salt, pepper and olive oil

lemon wedges, *to serve*

Part of the joy of jarred antipasti is that it takes very little effort to deliver something flavour-packed to your plate. I was intent on creating a nibble out of jarred artichoke hearts that didn't take too much effort, but still elevated them to giddy heights previously unseen in the sundries area of my store cupboard. Naturally, there was only one thing for it, and that was a brief swim in batter before getting sizzled in some hot oil. This is the ideal little nibble to be holding when you smugly swan out of the kitchen on a summer's day. Hand them out to your pals and eat them while they are still hot enough that your fingers burn a little in their greasy grasp. Wash down with an ice-cold beer.

1 Combine the feta, yoghurt and 2 tablespoons of olive oil in a tall measuring jug. Whizz with a stick blender until you have a really smooth sauce (alternatively, you could do this in a blender).

2 Finely chop most of your dill and your kalamata olives. Add these to your whipped feta mixture, and fold through so that all the bits are totally mixed in.

3 Drain the artichoke hearts, and pat them dry with paper towels.

4 Make the batter by sifting your plain flour, cornflour and baking powder into a bowl. Add 1 teaspoon of fine sea salt and stir so that all the ingredients are combined, then whisk in the sparkling water.

5 Pour the vegetable oil into a medium-sized saucepan so that it comes about a third of the way up the sides of the pan. Heat it over a medium heat so that it gently comes up to about 180°C. If you don't have a thermometer, carefully drop a little batter into the pan. If it sizzles, your oil is hot enough to begin cooking. If it browns too quickly, turn down the heat a little.

6 Place your batter bowl next to the hob. Dip your artichokes into the batter one at a time, then shake off the excess and carefully lower them into the oil, working in batches. Fry for 3 minutes, or until the batter is crisp and golden, then remove from the pan with a slotted spoon and transfer to a plate lined with paper towels. Sprinkle with a little flaky sea salt while they are still hot. Keep them warm while you fry the rest.

7 Swoosh your feta dip onto the side of your plate, or pop it in a small bowl, then pile up your crispy artichokes next to it. Sprinkle over the remaining dill leaves, then serve with lemon wedges for squeezing.

Midweek *Mood*

So much of my socialising in my twenties was about eating supper cross-legged on someone's living room floor after work. Friends arrive at different times, depending on when people can escape the office, arms laden with olives and wine, and you sit down with a meal and put the world to rights. The food is normally something prepared the night before, or thrown together when you are logged off for the day. It can be just as delicious as a fancier spread you may put together on the weekend, but these meals are often the ones we lack inspiration for. In this chapter, you will find a few ideas for lovely things that still feel really nourishing and special, even if it is a Tuesday, and even if you haven't had much time to plan.

Cauliflower Shawarma Bowls

Serves
4

Cook time
50 minutes

400g tin of chickpeas

1 large cauliflower

1 tbsp ground cumin

1 tsp hot smoked paprika

1 tsp ground turmeric

½ tsp ground cinnamon

½ red cabbage

juice of 1½ lemons

200g bulgur wheat

1 cucumber

300g tomatoes on the vine

1 red onion

½ small bunch of parsley

1½ tsp sumac

4 white pittas

60g tahini

1 garlic clove

jar of pickled green chillies,
plus 30ml of the pickling liquid

salt, pepper and olive oil

Tip

*You could pre-bake the
cauliflower and chickpeas
the night before eating, then
reheat in the oven or eat at
room temperature.*

*Like many people, I don't always treat my body with a lot of respect
when it comes to feeding it a balanced diet. 'No parents, no vegetables',
my friend Kate and I used to shriek every weekend when, Friday night
to Monday morning, we subsisted almost entirely on beer, sausage
sandwiches and crisps. Mondays, Tuesdays and Wednesdays needed to
be vegetable-packed to rebalance the score, and dinners like this one hit
the spot massively. You have many, many vegetables getting involved, the
crunch of a pitta chip and the garlicky tang of tahini dressing. Making this
for dinner is treating your body with the consideration it deserves after
taking a little beating. Give yourself a hug, and cook this. You deserve it.*

1   Preheat your oven to 210°C/190°C fan/gas mark 6½. Drain your
    chickpeas, then pat them dry with paper towels.

2   Cut your cauliflower into small florets, and the stalk into pieces of a
    similar size. Add these to a baking tray, along with your chickpeas,
    and sprinkle over the cumin, paprika, turmeric and cinnamon, as
    well as 1 teaspoon of salt and 20 twists of black pepper. Drizzle
    over 3 tablespoons of olive oil, then toss the cauliflower and
    chickpeas so that each piece is evenly coated. Bake for 40 minutes.

3   Meanwhile, prepare the cabbage. Very finely slice the cabbage with
    a sharp knife or vegetable peeler. Place in a bowl, and squeeze over
    two-thirds of the lemon juice. Sprinkle in ½ teaspoon of salt, then
    massage with your hands for a couple of minutes to lightly pickle.

4   Cook your bulgur wheat according to the packet instructions.

5   Finely dice the cucumber and tomatoes, then peel, halve and finely
    dice the red onion and finely chop the parsley. Toss these all
    together in a large bowl with 1 teaspoon of the sumac and season
    to taste with salt, giving it a good mix to combine it all together.

6   Cut your pitta into bite-sized triangular pieces and arrange on a
    large baking sheet. Drizzle over 2 tablespoons of olive oil and
    ½ teaspoon of salt, then pop in the oven for 8 minutes to crisp up.

7   Pour your tahini into a bowl. Squeeze in the remaining lemon juice,
    then grate in your garlic clove. Add the 30ml pickled chilli liquid,
    then whisk until smooth, loosening with water if necessary until
    you have a drizzleable consistency. Season to taste with salt.

8   Spoon your bulgur wheat into the bases of 4 bowls, then spoon in
    your cauliflower and chickpeas, pickled cabbage, diced veg and
    pitta chips. Add the pickled chillies, then drizzle over your tahini
    sauce, and sprinkle with the remaining sumac. Serve.

Zingy Chicken and Rice Broth

Serves
4

Cook time
1 hour

4 spring onions

4 garlic cloves

½ small bunch of coriander

1 cinnamon stick

1 star anise

1.2 litres chicken stock

2 tbsp fish sauce

750g chicken thighs and drumsticks *(bones in and skin on)*

200g jasmine rice

1 red chilli

juice of ½ lime, *plus wedges to serve*

salt, pepper and vegetable oil

The medicinal properties of a chicken broth make it an ideal supper for when you are feeling a little under the weather, either physically or emotionally. In our house, we often turn to a light broth of this nature when we have had a tough day, and it's also the perfect thing to feed any guests who are going through it a bit. Pop a friend down on the sofa with a big bowl of this broth, a box of tissues and an unlimited supply of hugs, and I defy them not to feel a little bit better afterwards.

1 Cut 2 of your spring onions into 4cm lengths. Bash 2 of your garlic cloves, then peel off their skins. Pick the leaves off your coriander, then finely slice the stalks.

2 Add the sliced spring onions, bashed garlic cloves and coriander stalks to a large pot over a low heat, along with your cinnamon stick and star anise. Pour in the chicken stock, followed by the fish sauce and ½ teaspoon of salt, then bring it to a gentle simmer. Add the chicken thighs and drumsticks to the pan, then simmer over a low heat for 30 minutes.

3 Tip the rice into a sieve, and give it a good rinse until the water runs clear.

4 Once the chicken broth has been simmering for 30 minutes, add the rice to the pan. Leave to simmer for 12 minutes.

5 Meanwhile, finely slice the chilli and the remaining garlic cloves and spring onions.

6 Heat 4 tablespoons of vegetable oil a small frying pan over a low-medium heat. Add the sliced chilli and garlic and fry for about 3 minutes, or until the garlic has turned a light golden colour and the chilli looks a bit frazzled. Remove the garlic and chilli from the oil with a slotted spoon, and leave them to drain on a plate lined with paper towels.

7 Take the broth off the heat. Remove the chicken from the pan and peel off the skin. Shred the meat off the bones with 2 forks, then return the shredded chicken to the broth. Squeeze in the lime juice, then season with more salt if needed.

8 Spoon the broth into bowls, then top with your crispy garlic and chilli, along with the coriander leaves and finely sliced spring onions. Serve with lime wedges on the side.

Burnt Aubergine Curry with Chickpea Pancakes

Serves
4

Cook time
1 hour, plus resting

2 aubergines

1 large onion

1 tbsp cumin seeds

160g gram flour

2 tsp garam masala

1 tsp ground turmeric

4 garlic cloves

3cm knob of ginger

1 tsp kashmiri chilli powder
(or mild chilli powder)

400g tin of chickpeas

400g tinned chopped tomatoes

150g coconut yoghurt

½ tsp caster sugar

½ small bunch of coriander,
leaves picked, to serve

salt and vegetable oil

Getting aubergines really soft can be tricky, but this method of charring them directly over a hot flame is a foolproof way of ensuring they collapse with the poke of a fork, and take on gorgeous smoky flavour. I often cook this curry midweek, as it takes very little time and mostly relies on a well-stocked store cupboard. The pancakes are the special bit that levels it up.

1 If you have a gas hob, turn 2 of the burners to a medium flame. Pop your aubergines over the flames, and cook them for about 10 minutes, rotating regularly. Alternatively, stab them all over with a fork and whack them under a very hot grill, or cook them on a barbecue. You want the skins to get charred and wrinkly, and the middle to be soft. Leave them to cool on a plate.

2 While your aubergines cook, peel and finely slice the onion. Heat 5 tablespoons of vegetable oil in a lidded casserole dish over a medium heat. Add the cumin seeds, and toast for a minute until they are fragrant, then add your sliced onion with a pinch of salt, and cook for about 15 minutes until it has softened and taken on a little colour.

3 When your aubergines are cool enough to handle, peel off the charred skins with your fingers, and shred the flesh with a fork.

4 To make the chickpea pancake batter, sift the gram flour into a medium-sized mixing bowl, then add 1 teaspoon of your garam masala, ½ teaspoon of turmeric and 1 teaspoon of salt. Make a well in the middle, then pour in 260ml water. Whisk together to create a smooth batter, then leave it to sit for 20 minutes.

5 Peel and finely chop the garlic and ginger and add to the curry pan, along with the chilli powder and the remaining teaspoon of garam masala and ½ teaspoon of turmeric. Cook for 2 minutes.

6 Drain the chickpeas in a colander. Tip the tinned tomatoes into the pan with the chickpeas and 120g of the coconut yoghurt. Add the aubergine flesh and sugar. Bring the mixture to the boil, then reduce the heat to as low as possible and simmer gently for 25 minutes.

7 When the curry has about 8 minutes left, make your pancakes. Heat 1 tablespoon of oil in a non-stick frying pan over a medium heat. Add a ladleful of batter, swirling the pan around to form a thin pancake. Cook for about a minute until nice and lacy, then flip it over and cook for another minute. Repeat with the remaining batter. Wrap your pancakes in a clean tea towel whilst you fry up the rest.

8 When everything is ready, season the curry to taste with salt. Pile the curry into the pancakes, then dollop on the remaining coconut yoghurt and scatter over the coriander leaves. Serve.

Sticky Tofu Spag Bol

Serves

4

Cook time

45 minutes

½ tsp Sichuan peppercorns

1 large onion

1 carrot

3 garlic cloves

4 spring onions

300g firm tofu

2 tbsp dark soy sauce

3 tbsp tomato purée

250g soba noodles

2 tbsp cornflour

For the sauce

4 tbsp Shaoxing rice wine

2 tbsp dark soy sauce

2 tbsp light soy sauce

2 tbsp crispy chilli oil

1 tsp caster sugar

salt, pepper and vegetable oil

A midweek meals chapter would be incomplete without noodles, everyone's favourite speedy dinner staple. This isn't really a spag bol at all, but it does look like one. Crumbling tofu to a mince-like texture is one of my favourite ways to eat it. It's simmered with a tingly, spicy sauce with a sofrito base and tossed with noodles, hence the spag bol likeness. I haven't gone crazy on the spice here, but by all means, amp it up if you are a spice fiend. Bar a couple of pieces of veg and a block of tofu, this recipe relies almost entirely on store-cupboard bits, making it an ideal thing to throw together when you are too short on time to run to the shops, and are looking for something flavour-packed and satisfying.

1 Tip your Sichuan peppercorns into a large sauté pan set over a medium-high heat. Toast for 2 minutes until fragrant, then bash them to a powder using a pestle and mortar.

2 Peel and finely chop your onion, carrot and garlic. Cut your spring onions into 1cm lengths, discarding any tough and woody ends.

3 Bring a medium-sized saucepan of salted water to the boil.

4 Heat 2 tablespoons of vegetable oil in the sauté pan over a medium-high heat. Crumble in your tofu with your hands; it should resemble mince. Add ½ teaspoon of salt, then fry for 5 minutes until the tofu is golden and crisp all over. Add 2 tablespoons of your dark soy sauce, and reduce for 2 minutes so your tofu darkens in colour. Remove the tofu from the pan with a slotted spoon.

5 Add 4 tablespoons of vegetable oil to the pan and reduce the heat to medium. Add the onion, carrot and spring onion, and fry for about 10 minutes until softened.

6 Meanwhile, combine the sauce ingredients in a bowl and mix well.

7 Add your tomato purée to the mixture in the pan and cook for 3 minutes until darkened, then add the garlic. Tip the tofu back into the sauté pan, then pour in the sauce. Give it a mix to combine.

8 Cook your soba noodles in the saucepan of boiling water according to the packet instructions.

9 In a small bowl, mix the cornflour with 2 tablespoons of water to make a paste. Add 300ml water to the pan, then tip in your cornflour paste. Mix to combine, then reduce the heat to low and let it simmer for 2 minutes. The sauce should get thick and shiny.

10 Drain your noodles, add them to the pan and give it a good mix. Check the seasoning – the soy should have it nice and salty, but it's always good to check! Tong your noodles into bowls and serve.

Creamy Sausage, Leek and Bean Stew

Serves
4

Cook time
1 hour

2 large leeks

4 garlic cloves

a few thyme sprigs

200ml white wine

200ml chicken stock

1 large posh jar of butter beans
(or 2 × 400g tins)

12 good-quality pork sausages

260g spinach

40g breadcrumbs *(panko or fresh would be fine)*

2 tbsp crème fraîche

20g Parmesan

zest of 1 lemon and juice of ½

salt, pepper and olive oil

I posted a video online for this dish a couple of years back, and it blew up more than I could have imagined a humble bowl of pulses ever might. I am a bean and sausage superfan, but I had no idea that so many other people would be equally enthusiastic about them. We are living through a bean revolution, and I am here for it! This is a version of a dish that I have cooked repeatedly over the years, swapping in different vegetables for different seasons. You could use any dark, leafy green in place of spinach – and a veggie sausage would not go amiss here instead of a porky one, if that's your thing.

1   Finely slice the leeks. Peel and chop the garlic.

2   Heat 4 tablespoons of olive oil in a large casserole dish over a medium heat. Add the chopped leeks, along with ½ teaspoon of salt, and cook for 10 minutes until they are totally soft. Add your garlic and pick in your thyme leaves, then give it a stir and cook for a further 2 minutes.

3   Add the wine and cook for another 3 minutes to let it reduce right down. Pour in your chicken stock and beans, as well as the bean liquid. Stir to combine, then reduce the heat to low and cover the pot with a lid. Simmer for 15 minutes.

4   Meanwhile, heat 1 tablespoon of olive oil in a frying pan over a medium-high heat. Add the sausages and fry for 5 minutes until you get a nice char on the outside – they won't be cooked all the way through, but you just want to get some colour on them.

5   Add the spinach to the bean mixture in the casserole, then place the sausages on top. Turn the heat right down, then pop a lid on the pan and leave it to simmer for 15 minutes.

6   Meanwhile, tip the breadcrumbs into the same pan the sausages were cooked in, and fry them over a medium heat for 3 minutes until they are lightly browned and crispy. The bread will soak up all that delicious sausage flavour to create a crispy topping.

7   Remove the lid from the casserole dish and stir in the crème fraîche. Grate in the Parmesan and lemon zest, then add the lemon juice. Season to taste with salt and 10 twists of pepper.

8   Spoon your stew into bowls, then sprinkle over the breadcrumbs and serve.

Tofu Traybake Tacos

Serves

6

Cook time

1 hour, plus soaking

2 dried chipotle chillies

2 tsp cumin seeds

1 tsp coriander seeds

2 red onions

3 mixed peppers *(not green)*

3 garlic cloves

2 tbsp tomato purée

1 tsp hot smoked paprika

600g firm tofu

400g tinned chopped tomatoes

400g tin of black beans

small bunch of coriander

1 green chilli

100g silken tofu

juice of 1 lime

18 corn tortillas

salt, pepper and olive oil

Traybake dinners are so damn satisfying. The mountains of washing-up that often come with making a taco-based dinner can put you off making them altogether. All you need for this is two baking trays, a pestle and mortar and a chopping board, so you can spend less of your evening precariously stacking pans in the sink, and more time on the margs.

1 Preheat your oven to 200°C/180°C fan/gas mark 6.

2 Cut the stalks off your chillies and shake out the seeds. Toast in a dry frying pan over a medium heat for a few minutes until fragrant, then pop them into a small bowl and pour over about 150ml boiling water, or just enough to cover them. Leave to soak for 30 minutes.

3 In the same small frying pan, toast your cumin and coriander seeds over a medium heat for 1 minute until they are fragrant. Bash them to a fine powder using a pestle and mortar.

4 Peel and halve your onions. Finely slice your onions and peppers, discarding the stalks and any seeds. Peel and finely chop your garlic. Tip the peppers, onions and garlic into a large baking dish. Add the tomato purée, along with the toasted spices, the paprika, 3 tablespoons of olive oil, and 1 teaspoon of salt. Bake for 30 minutes, stirring every so often so that they cook evenly.

5 Grate your tofu and put on a baking sheet. Drizzle over 2 tablespoons of olive oil and 1 teaspoon of salt. Bake for 30 minutes until crispy.

6 Meanwhile, remove your chipotle peppers from their liquid and roughly chop, then bash to a rough paste using a pestle and mortar. Drain the black beans and give them a rinse.

7 After 30 minutes, remove the veg baking dish and the tofu from the oven. Add your tofu into the veg baking dish, followed by the tinned tomatoes, black beans, chipotle paste and 1 teaspoon of salt. Give it a mix, then return to the oven for another 15 minutes.

8 Meanwhile, finely chop the coriander, leaves, stalks and all, and your green chilli. Add them to a pestle and mortar, and bash to a paste. Add the silken tofu, lime juice and 20ml water, then give it all a mix until you have a thick sauce. Season this to taste with salt.

9 Heat your tortillas over a flame for 10 seconds on each side, or in a hot dry frying pan. Wrap in a clean tea towel to keep them warm.

10 Preheat your grill to high and pop your tofu mix under it for 3 minutes to crisp up the top a little. Season it to taste with more salt, if needed, then pop the baking dish on the table with your bowl of salsa and tortillas on plates, for everyone to serve themselves.

Chipotle Tomatoes with White Beans and Feta

Serves
2

Cook time
25 minutes

1 large red onion

3 garlic cloves

250g cherry tomatoes
on the vine

juice of 1 lime

1 tsp cumin seeds

400g tin of cannellini beans

1 tbsp sour cream

1 tsp chipotle paste (*I like
the Gran Luchito one*)

½ small bunch of coriander

50g feta

salt, pepper and olive oil

Bean-based meals are a staple of my midweek life. They provide a perfect blank canvas for loads of flavours and ingredients, depending on the season and my mood. This is a dreamy way to eat them in the summer months. Sweet little tomatoes are the belle of the season: delicious on their own, but also capable of holding some pretty bold flavours, like the smoky chipotle paste here. Onions are a waste of space when not properly cooked – if they're crunchy and raw in the middle, yet slightly burnt on the outside, they add nothing. By adding splashes of water to the pan, you can speed up what can be a tedious process, and get dinner on the table quicker.

1   Peel and finely slice your onion and garlic, then halve your cherry tomatoes.

2   Add a quarter of your sliced onions to a small bowl. Squeeze over half the lime juice, as well as ½ teaspoon of salt, then scrunch them up to lightly pickle them.

3   Heat 2 tablespoons of olive oil in a frying pan over a medium heat. Tip in your cumin seeds and toast them for 1 minute until fragrant.

4   Add the remaining sliced onions to the pan, and fry for 15 minutes until they have totally softened. If it looks like they are catching on the bottom of the ban, add a little splash of water – this will help to steam and soften them.

5   Drain your cannellini beans and give them a rinse. In a separate frying pan, heat 2 tablespoons of olive oil over a medium heat. Add half the garlic and fry for a minute until fragrant, but don't let it brown.

6   Tip in your drained cannellini beans, along with 100ml water, and bring the mixture to a gentle simmer. Cook for 5 minutes, squishing about half the beans down with your wooden spoon as you go to create a creamy texture. Add the sour cream, then season the beans to taste with salt and 10 twists of pepper. Set aside and keep warm.

7   Once your onions are soft, add the remaining garlic to the pan. Cook for 1 minute, then tip in the cherry tomatoes. Fry for 5 minutes, bursting a few of the tomatoes with the back of your spoon to get it nice and saucy.

8   Squeeze in the remaining lime juice, then stir in the chipotle paste. Season to taste with salt. Roughly chop the coriander.

9   Spoon your cannellini beans into bowls, then top with your saucy tomatoes. Crumble over some feta, and sprinkle on your pickled onions and chopped coriander to serve.

Sticky Mushroom Skewer Bowls

Serves
4

Cook time
1 hour, plus soaking
and marinating

For the rice
300g sushi rice

1 tsp rice vinegar

For the mushrooms
1 tsp ground cumin

4 tbsp light soy sauce

2 tbsp dark soy sauce

1 tsp caster sugar

2 tsp sesame oil

500g king oyster mushrooms

2 tbsp sesame seeds, *to serve*

1 tbsp shichimi togarashi
(optional, to serve)

2 tbsp pickled sushi ginger
(optional, to serve)

For the smacked cucumber
1 cucumber

1 garlic clove

2 tbsp light soy sauce

1 tsp rice vinegar

1 tsp crispy chilli oil

2 tbsp tahini

½ tsp caster sugar

**You will need 8 wooden
or metal skewers**

Admittedly, this meal takes a little more time to prepare than others in this chapter, as sushi rice is a rather particular customer who requires rather particular treatment, but it is worth it for a steaming bowl of food that makes you feel seriously nourished. This dish is another example of me being staunchly in the Oyster Mushroom Fan Club (you will find many examples of this in the pages of this book). Marinating them in umami-rich soy before grilling them makes them look alarmingly like a chicken kebab, and the chew? Phenomenal. This is a bowl of food to cook when you are in your Clean Girl Era*, and want to spread the joy of feeling like a healthy goddess.

* I say this with irony – this is a very occasional feeling that comes over me on a day where I don't consume an entire packet of crumpets. There is no such thing as 'Clean' or 'Dirty' food.

1   Soak 8 wooden skewers in water overnight to stop them burning when they cook. Alternatively, you could use metal skewers.

2   Tip your sushi rice into a large bowl, and pour in enough cold water to cover it. Swish it around in the water with your hands – the water will become cloudy – then drain it in a sieve. Repeat this step 5 times, or until the water in the bowl stays clear when you've swirled the rice around. Pour the rice back into the bowl, cover it with fresh water, and leave it to soak for 20 minutes.

3   Prep your mushroom skewers. In a bowl, combine the cumin, soy sauces, caster sugar, sesame oil and 4 tablespoons of water, and give it a whisk to combine. Slice your mushroom stalks into discs 3mm thick, and tear the heads into pieces of a similar size. Add your mushroom slices to the marinade, and give it a stir so they are totally coated. You could do this in the morning and leave to marinate all day, or just for 30 minutes.

4   Make your smacked cucumber. Place the cucumber on a chopping board, and bash it with the base of a pan or a rolling pin to break it up a bit, then chop into chunks of around 2cm. Add it to a bowl, then sprinkle over 1 teaspoon of salt. Let it sit for 10 minutes while you peel and finely chop the garlic.

5   Drain any water off your cucumber, then add the garlic, soy sauce, rice vinegar, chilli oil, tahini and caster sugar to the bowl and give it a good mix.

continues overleaf

Sticky Mushroom Skewer Bowls

6 Tip your sushi rice into a large saucepan with a lid, then pour in 390ml cold water. Place it over a high heat and bring to the boil. Pop on a lid, reduce the heat to very low, and simmer for 15 minutes.

7 Leaving the lid on, remove your rice from the heat and let it sit for another 15 minutes.

8 Thread your mushroom slices onto 8 skewers, making sure they are compact. Fold some of your mushroom pieces over before skewering them, to create irregular shapes.

9 Heat a cast-iron skillet or frying pan over a medium-high heat. Add your mushroom skewers and briefly press them down with the lid of a pan. Cook for about 8 minutes, rotating them frequently so they cook evenly, and occasionally brushing them with any marinade left in the bowl.

10 Toast your sesame seeds in a dry frying pan over a medium heat for 3 minutes, or until they are lovely and golden.

11 Once the rice has been resting for 15 minutes, remove the lid, then add the vinegar and fluff it up with a fork.

12 Spoon your rice into bowls. Top with your mushroom skewers and smacked cucumber salad, the toasted sesame seeds, plus your shichimi togarashi and sushi ginger, if you're using them. Serve.

Tip

By all means, use a different type of rice if you prefer to speed things along, but the stickiness of sushi rice is unrivalled here.

Spinachy Lentils with Sticky Tamarind Paneer

Serves
4

Cook time
1 hour

300g red split lentils

2 onions

20g butter

1 tbsp cumin seeds

5cm knob of ginger

5 garlic cloves

3 red chillies

250g paneer

2 tsp garam masala

1 tsp ground turmeric

2 tbsp tomato purée

400g frozen whole-leaf spinach

3 tbsp tamarind sauce
(I like the Maggi one)

½ small bunch of coriander

salt and vegetable oil

Tip

The lentil base freezes beautifully; I'd highly recommend freezing a few portions for future you to enjoy.

There is no meal I crave more frequently than a good old-fashioned dal. It is phenomenally cheap to make, as well as being so soothing and nourishing. If it is just me on a Monday night, I cook up a steaming bowl of this. To zhuzh it up a bit when you have company, I've topped it with some sticky tamarind paneer and jammy onions. This is a midweek staple if I ever saw one, but is very much delicious enough to feed to a friend.

1 Tip your lentils into a sieve and rinse them under a cold tap until the water runs clear. Transfer to a medium-sized saucepan, and add 1.2 litres cold water. Pop the pan over a medium heat and bring it to a boil. Skim off the scum with a spoon, then reduce the heat to low and simmer your lentils for 30 minutes.

2 Meanwhile, peel and finely slice the onions. Heat a large sauté pan over a medium heat. Add the butter, followed by the cumin seeds, and cook for 2 minutes until fragrant. Tip in your onions and cook for 15 minutes, until they have softened and taken on a little colour.

3 While your onions cook, peel and finely chop the ginger and garlic. Finely chop 2 of the red chillies, seeds and all, and slice the third.

4 Cut your paneer into 2cm cubes and tip these into a bowl. Sprinkle over 1 teaspoon of the garam masala and ½ teaspoon of the turmeric, as well as 1 tablespoon of vegetable oil and ½ teaspoon of salt. Toss it all to combine, then set it aside to marinate for a bit.

5 Remove 2 tablespoons of your onions from the pan, setting them aside. Add the tomato purée, garlic, ginger and chopped chillies to the onions still in the pan and cook these for 3 minutes until the colour has darkened. Stir in the remaining ½ teaspoon of turmeric and 1 teaspoon of garam masala, and cook for 2 minutes more.

6 Preheat your grill to high and line a baking tray with kitchen foil.

7 Add the spinach to the lentil pan, along with 150ml water. Bring it to a simmer, and cook gently for 5 minutes, or until it has defrosted.

8 Tip the paneer into the baking tray, and place under the grill for 5 minutes, turning the pieces occasionally so they char evenly. Remove the paneer from under the grill, and drizzle it all over with the tamarind sauce. Toss it around so that it's all coated.

9 Add half of your spinach-and-onion mixture to a blender and blitz until smooth. Pour this into the pan of lentils, followed by the rest of the spinach mixture, and season to taste with salt.

10 Spoon your lentils into bowls and top with your sticky paneer, the sliced chilli, remaining onions and coriander leaves. Serve.

All the Greens Fried Rice with Crispy Sesame Egg

Serves
4

Cook time
30 minutes

2 banana shallots

3 garlic cloves

2 lemongrass stalks

2–3 green chillies, *depending how spicy you like it*

2cm knob of ginger

½ small bunch of coriander

2 tbsp desiccated coconut

2 tsp fish sauce

zest and juice of 1 lime

200g Tenderstem broccoli

150g green beans

2 spring onions

600g cooked jasmine rice
(this is best cooked a day in advance)

2 tbsp sesame seeds

4 eggs

2 tbsp soy sauce

salt, pepper and vegetable oil

Tip

If you want to prep ahead of time, the paste keeps for a week in the fridge and can even be frozen.

Cooking fried rice is a tradition so rooted in East Asian culture that I would not claim to be an expert in it, and this version isn't authentic to any place other than my kitchen. It's inspired by one I ate in Thailand, when my friend Martha was low on cash, and ate rice with a crispy fried egg on top twice a day for weeks. I followed suit occasionally when I needed simple comfort, and stumbled across a dish similar to this one in Krabi. The rice had been fried in a green curry paste, making it aromatic and spicy, and was topped with a lacy fried egg with a particularly crispy bottom. This recipe uses a simplified version of green curry paste, for busy cooks without access to some of the more hard-to-come-by ingredients.

1 Start by making your curry paste. Peel your shallots and garlic, then roughly chop them. Bash your lemongrass stalks with the flat side of your knife to break them up a bit, then discard any woody parts and finely chop the rest. Finely chop your chillies and ginger, too, as well as your coriander stalks.

2 Add all these ingredients to a small food processor, along with your desiccated coconut, fish sauce, 1 teaspoon of salt and 2 tablespoons of vegetable oil. Zest in your lime, then whizz it all to a smooth paste. You may need to scrape down the sides occasionally to make sure it all gets incorporated.

3 Cut your broccoli and green beans into 3cm lengths, and finely slice your spring onions.

4 Heat 3 tablespoons of vegetable oil in a wok over a medium heat. Tip in your broccoli and green beans and fry for 4 minutes until they have softened and taken on colour. Stir in the curry paste, and fry for another 4 minutes until it is fragrant and ceases to smell raw.

5 Tip in the cooked rice and stir-fry for 3 minutes so that the paste totally coats the rice grains, and everything is steaming hot.

6 While your rice fries, get your eggs cooking. Heat 6 tablespoons of vegetable oil in a large non-stick frying pan over a high heat. Add the spring onions and sesame seeds, and cook for 30 seconds. The spring onions should sizzle, and the sesame seeds should just start to take on colour. Crack in your eggs and let them fry for 2 minutes, sprinkling the surfaces with a little salt. They should crackle, bubble and hiss, and build up a really crispy base. Tilt your pan and flick the oil over the top of the egg whites with a spoon to cook them.

7 Stir the soy sauce and lime juice into the rice, then season to taste with salt. Spoon into bowls, and top each bowl with a crispy fried egg and some coriander leaves. Serve.

Harissa Braised Cod and Giant Couscous

Serves
4

Cook time
40 minutes

1 large onion

1 red pepper

4 garlic cloves

400g cherry tomatoes

1 tsp ground cumin

1 tsp ground coriander

½ tsp ground cinnamon

2 tbsp rose harissa paste

400ml vegetable stock

225g giant couscous

600g cod loin

small bunch of parsley

1 lemon

salt, pepper and olive oil

This is a dish I first cooked at my friend Tom's family house in Devon. We'd spent a scorcher of a day stomping along the cliffs, swimming in the sea and eating sandwiches while wrapped up in our beach towels. I cooked this dish for dinner with veg from the garden when we got home, and our salty skin and rosy cheeks were nourished by steaming bowls of soft white fish poached in a lightly spiced tomato broth. It's a simple one to rustle up on a summer's evening, and would be equally soul-soothing in the depths of winter – although you may want to swap out the fresh cherry tomatoes for tinned ones in this instance.

1   Peel, halve and finely slice your onion. Finely slice your red pepper too, discarding all the seeds and the stem.

2   Heat 4 tablespoons of olive oil in a large sauté pan over a medium heat. Add the onion and pepper, and cook for 15–20 minutes until really soft.

3   While the onion and pepper are cooking, peel and finely chop your garlic. Halve your cherry tomatoes.

4   Add the garlic to the pan, along with the ground spices, and cook for 2 minutes until fragrant. Tip your cherry tomatoes into the pan and squish them up a bit with your spoon. Cook for 5 minutes until they are nice and jammy, then add the harissa paste and vegetable stock, and bring the mixture to a simmer. Season with ½ teaspoon of salt, reduce the heat to low and leave to simmer gently while you prep the rest.

5   Bring a medium-sized saucepan of water to a boil. Add the couscous and simmer for 8 minutes until tender.

6   Meanwhile, cut your cod loin into large chunks, about 5cm big. Nestle these fish chunks into your sauté pan with all the veg, then reduce the heat to low. Pop a lid on the pan and let it gently poach for 7–8 minutes. The fish should turn opaque and easily flake when it is cooked, but you don't want the pieces to fall apart too much.

7   While the fish is cooking, roughly chop the parsley and cut the lemon into wedges.

8   Once your fish is cooked, drain the couscous and tip this into the pan around the fish, then season the broth to taste. Ladle everything into bowls, then scatter with the chopped parsley. Serve with lemon wedges for squeezing.

Sausage, Squash and Taleggio Traybake

Serves
5

Cook time
1 hour

1 large butternut squash

1 large onion

1 tsp chilli flakes

2 rosemary sprigs

10 good-quality pork sausages

75g cornichons

small bunch of parsley

juice of ½ lemon

100g whole-leaf kale

120g ciabatta

200g Taleggio

salt, pepper and olive oil

The hill I would happily die on is one emblazoned with a big billboard that says: 'Sausages are the singular best food item in the world.' I love them with mash; I love them squished up into pasta sauce; I love them cold from the fridge the day after a barbecue, with a lovely thick char on them. This one-tray dish, packed with autumnal veg, is a particularly comforting way to eat them. Taleggio is a soft and funky cheese that I think makes a spectacular match for the sweet roasted squash chunks and earthy kale. Spreading it out over two trays means that the squash and sausages all get a good kiss of heat from the oven, getting them all burnished and lovely.

1 Preheat your oven to 220°C/200°C fan/gas mark 7.

2 Halve your squash, remove the seeds and cut the flesh into slices 2cm thick. Peel and halve your onion, then chop it into wedges, leaving the root intact so that the wedges don't break apart.

3 Arrange the squash and onion pieces over 2 large baking trays. Drizzle each tray with 2 tablespoons of olive oil, the chilli flakes and a teaspoon of salt. Pull your rosemary leaves off the sprigs, and spread these around the trays too. Add the sausages to the trays, then bake for 35 minutes, turning everything halfway through.

4 Meanwhile, finely slice the cornichons and chop the parsley. Add these to a bowl and squeeze in the lemon juice. Add 3 tablespoons of olive oil, and give the whole thing a good mix.

5 Pull the kale leaves off their stalks and tear the leaves into bite-sized pieces, then add them to a bowl with 1 tablespoon of olive oil and ½ teaspoon of salt. Give it all a good toss with your hands to coat the kale in the oil. Tear the ciabatta into bite-sized pieces and slice the Taleggio; it is a very soft cheese, so it may break apart, but that's okay.

6 Once the sausages and squash have been in the oven for 35 minutes, nestle the ciabatta pieces into the trays and drizzle them with a little oil, then return to the oven for 5 minutes.

7 Now add the kale to the trays, and arrange the Taleggio slices over the top. Bake for another 5 minutes.

8 To serve, spoon the cornichon salsa over the top and dig in.

Coconut Chicken and Bean Salad
with Jammy Shallots

Serves
2

Cook time
45 minutes

4 chicken thighs
(bones in and skin on)

3 banana shallots

2 tbsp fish sauce

2 tbsp red wine vinegar

2½ tsp caster sugar

200g green beans

1 garlic clove

2 red chillies

150ml full-fat coconut milk

zest and juice of 1 lime

½ small bunch of coriander

salt, pepper and olive oil

A warm chicken salad is a very lovely thing. Chicken fat is one of the most gorgeous naturally occurring flavours in the world, I reckon. Cooking chicken thighs skin-side down in a frying pan means releasing all that flavour, which can then be sponged up by whatever you cook in the juices. In this case, you cook some jammy shallots in the fat, then toss them with that crispy chicken and some tender green beans to make a very fragrant salad situation. You could even double up and save some for your lunch the next day.

1 Debone your chicken thighs by carefully slicing on either side of the bones, and scraping the flesh down it to release them. Season all over with salt.

2 Place a frying pan over a medium heat and add the chicken thighs to the pan while it is still cool, placing them skin-side down. Pop a square of baking parchment over the chicken, then top with a heavy pan. This will ensure you get really crispy skin. Fry for 10 minutes.

3 Meanwhile, peel and quarter your shallots lengthways, keeping the stems intact and removing any tough bits.

4 Remove the heavy pan and parchment from the chicken. Flip each thigh over and fry for another 5 minutes on the other side. Remove the chicken from the pan and set aside to cool. There should be lots of delicious chicken fat left in the pan.

5 Add your shallots to the chicken pan, cut-side down. Fry for 4 minutes to get a little char on them, then flip and fry for another 2 minutes on the other side.

6 Add 100ml water, along with the fish sauce, red wine vinegar and 1½ teaspoons of the sugar. Put the piece of baking parchment you used earlier on top, and reduce the heat to low. Let it all bubble down for 5 minutes to soften the shallots. They should get nice and sticky. Remove the paper and spoon any leftover juices over the shallots, then remove the pan from the heat.

7 Heat 1 tablespoon of olive oil in a separate frying pan over a medium-high heat. Add the green beans, and fry for about 5 minutes until they are tender and slightly charred.

continues overleaf

Coconut Chicken and Bean Salad with Jammy Shallots

8 Meanwhile, make your dressing. Peel your garlic, and finely chop the garlic and one of your red chillies, then scrape these into a small saucepan. Pour in your coconut milk, then place over a medium heat for about 5 minutes to reduce by half.

9 Remove from the heat and let it cool. Add the lime zest and juice, along with the remaining 1 teaspoon of sugar. Give it a mix, and season to taste with salt.

10 Pick your coriander leaves and slice your chicken. Finely slice the remaining red chilli.

11 Tip the green beans, coriander leaves and shallots into a mixing bowl, then pour over your dressing. Toss together to combine.

12 Divide your salad between 2 plates, then top with the crispy chicken. Serve with the sliced red chilli on top.

Lamb and Charred Pepper Beans

Serves
4

Cook time
1 hour

1 aubergine

2 red peppers

1 onion

4 garlic cloves

3 tbsp tomato purée

1 tbsp sweet smoked paprika

1½ tsp ground cumin

1 large posh jar of butter beans
(or 2 × 400g tins)

400ml chicken stock

1 tbsp red wine vinegar

½ small bunch of parsley

500g lamb mince
(20 per cent fat)

For the tahini sauce
80g tahini

juice of ½ lemon

salt and olive oil

Another day, another beany dinner. This one is a bold and smoky affair, making the most of summer vegetables. It takes inspiration from all over the shop, borrowing an Ajvar-esque base from Serbia, and tahini from the Levant. Ajvar is a Serbian dip made with aubergines and peppers cooked over a barbecue, and the smokiness is killer with lamb. I wanted to make this a dish you would also cook on a rainy day, so this method doesn't require a barbecue, but if you are so inclined, you can absolutely use one.

1   If you have a gas hob, turn 3 of the burners to a medium flame. Pop your aubergine and peppers directly over the flames, and cook them for about 10 minutes, rotating them regularly so that they cook evenly. Alternatively, you could whack them under a very hot grill, or cook them on a barbecue. You want the skins to get very charred and wrinkly, and the flesh to be soft. Leave them to cool on a plate.

2   Peel, halve and finely slice your onion. Peel and finely chop your garlic. Heat 4 tablespoons of olive oil in a sauté pan over a medium-low heat. Add the onion and cook for 15 minutes until totally soft.

3   Once the aubergine and peppers are cool enough to handle, peel off their skins and discard. Remove the seeds from inside the peppers, and discard these too. Add the flesh of the aubergine and peppers to a food processor, and whizz to form a paste.

4   Add the tomato purée, garlic, smoked paprika and 1 teaspoon of the ground cumin to the pan with the onions, and cook for 5 minutes until the tomato purée has darkened and is starting to stick to the pan.

5   Drain your beans and give them a rinse, then tip them into the pan, along with your aubergine and pepper paste, chicken stock and vinegar. Bring the mixture to the boil, then reduce the heat to low and leave to simmer for 20 minutes. Season to taste with salt.

6   While your beans simmer, make the sauce. In a bowl, combine the tahini with the lemon juice and 60ml water, and whisk. It will look split and thick, but keep going and it will come together smoothly – you want it to be a drizzle-able consistency. Season to taste with salt.

7   Roughly chop the parsley.

8   Heat another large sauté pan over a medium heat, and add your lamb mince. Season with your remaining ½ teaspoon of ground cumin and 1 teaspoon of salt, then break up the mince with your spoon. Fry for 5 minutes until crispy, then take off the heat.

9   Spoon your beans into bowls, and top them with the crispy lamb mince and tahini sauce. Sprinkle over the parsley and serve.

Peanutty Gochujang Prawn Noodles

Serves

2

Cook time

20 minutes

4 spring onions

1 red pepper

2 garlic cloves

2cm knob of ginger

2 tbsp peanut butter *(smooth or chunky – whatever your preference)*

1 tbsp gochujang

1 tsp light soy sauce

2 tsp dark soy sauce

½ tsp caster sugar

165g peeled raw king prawns

400g udon noodles

salt and vegetable oil

When I went to university, I considered myself quite the culinary mastermind. I thought I was the next Heston Blumenthal, cooking up VERY advanced meals like tricolore salads, arancini and teriyaki salmon (fancy!). One of my favourite innovations was peanut butter noodles, and this is my ode to that dish. This dish has only three fresh components – prawns, red pepper and spring onions – and the rest is a dry store party. Gochujang is a Korean condiment that you can get in lots of big supermarkets nowadays, but I recommend seeking out the one in a red clip-up box that you find in most Asian supermarkets. Nineteen-year-old Sophie would not believe the advancements we've made.

1 Finely slice your spring onions and red pepper. Peel and finely chop your garlic and ginger.

2 In a small bowl, combine the peanut butter, gochujang, both soy sauces and caster sugar with 3 tablespoons of water and give it all a good mix. This is your sauce – set it aside until later.

3 Heat 1 tablespoon of vegetable oil in a wok over a medium-high heat. Add the prawns and fry for 2 minutes until they have curled up and turned pink. Remove them from the pan and set aside.

4 Add another tablespoon of vegetable oil to the wok. Reserve about a teaspoon of spring onion greens for later, then add the rest of the chopped spring onions to the pan, along with the red pepper strips. Fry these for 3 minutes until they have softened, then add your garlic and ginger, and cook for 30 seconds more.

5 Tip your udon noodles into the pan, along with 100ml water to help them soften. Cook for 4 minutes until the block has broken apart and the noodles are tender.

6 Return the prawns to the pan, then add your sauce. Give it a really good toss to combine all your ingredients and warm them through.

7 Tong your noodles into bowls, then sprinkle with your reserved spring onion greens and serve.

Harissa Pepper Soup with Halloumi Croutons

Serves
4

Cook time
1 hour 10 minutes

1 large onion

3 garlic cloves

3 red peppers

140g red lentils

1 tsp ground cinnamon

1 tsp ground cumin

1 litre vegetable stock

½ bunch of parsley

zest and juice of 1 lemon

225g halloumi

1 tbsp rose harissa paste

salt, pepper and olive oil

Every Saturday growing up, lunch in the Wyburd house would have a similar theme. There would be a spread of cheeses, hams, sausage rolls, bread, possibly a salad, and always a soup. My mum is the queen of soups – she made one often that we coined Crying Soup, because it once moved my sister Phoebe to tears, she liked it so much. I can only hope that this spiced pepper number with squeaky, salty halloumi chunks might continue the great Wyburd family tradition of soups and induce strong emotions for you, too. The joy of dropping halloumi croutons into soup is that they stay hot, keeping them soft and chewy, rather than turning into crusty little bullets, as they are wont to do when allowed to cool down.

1 Peel and finely slice your onion and garlic. Finely slice your red peppers too, discarding all the seeds and stalks.

2 Heat 3 tablespoons of olive oil in a large saucepan over a medium heat. Tip in your onions and peppers, and fry them for about 20 minutes until they are totally softened and starting to caramelise.

3 Pour your lentils into a sieve, and give them a really good rinse under cold running water, until the water runs clear.

4 Add the garlic, cinnamon and cumin to the pan, and cook for 2 minutes, then tip in your lentils and vegetable stock. Bring to a simmer and leave to simmer gently for 30 minutes, or until the lentils are tender.

5 Meanwhile, finely chop your parsley. Bash to a paste using a pestle and mortar. Add the lemon zest and juice, along with 2 tablespoons of olive oil. Keep bashing until you have a little green sauce.

6 Slice your halloumi into 2cm chunks.

7 Once your lentils are cooked, pour the soup into a blender and add the harissa paste. Whizz until smooth. You may need to do this in a few batches. Alternatively, you could blitz it with a stick blender.

8 Pour the smooth soup back into the pan and season to taste with salt and 10 twists of black pepper. Keep the pan on a gentle simmer.

9 Heat a frying pan over a medium heat. Add your halloumi chunks and fry them for a few minutes on each side until they are golden all over.

10 Ladle your soup into bowls, and serve topped with your halloumi croutons and parsley oil.

Bombay Mix Chicken with Tamarind Broccoli

Serves
4

Cook time
1 hour

2 chicken breasts

75g Bombay mix,
plus 20g for the topping

55g panko breadcrumbs

100g plain flour

3 tbsp curry powder

2 eggs

200g thick natural yoghurt

1 tbsp hot sauce

400g Tenderstem broccoli

1 onion

4 garlic cloves

4 tbsp tamarind sauce
(I like the Maggi one)

lime wedges, *to serve*

salt, pepper and rapeseed oil

Tip
You could prep the chicken a day in advance for ease, then pan-fry it when you are ready to serve.

I'm not sure there is a snack more addictive than Bombay mix. A very clever person once told me to eat it from a mug so that you can pour it directly into your mouth for speed, and I have never looked back. My love for the stuff reached a point where I started incorporating it into actual meals by whizzing it up in a food processor, and using it as a crispy coating for fried little morsels. It works a treat on homemade fish fingers, even better on a chicken escalope. Serving it up with garlicky broccoli in a tangy tamarind sauce makes for a really special midweek dinner.

1   Prep your chicken. Halve each chicken breast through the centre so that you have two slim cutlets. Lay these pieces flat under a piece of cling film, and bash with a rolling pin to make them thin and even.

2   Pour 75g of your Bombay mix into a food processor and whizz it up to a fine powder. Pour this into a bowl and add your panko breadcrumbs. Mix to combine.

3   Tip your flour into a second bowl, and season with 1 tablespoon of the curry powder and 1 teaspoon of salt. Crack your eggs into a third bowl and beat them.

4   Dip your chicken pieces into the flour, then the egg, then the Bombay mix, ensuring they are totally coated. Set aside.

5   In a small bowl, mix the yoghurt, hot sauce and 2 tablespoons of curry powder. Trim the woody bits off the end of the broccoli stems.

6   Peel and finely slice your onion and garlic. Heat 3 tablespoons of rapeseed oil in a large skillet or griddle pan over a medium heat. Add the onion and garlic, and fry them for 15 minutes until softened and starting to crisp up a little. Remove from the pan and set aside. Add your broccoli to the pan, and fry for 5 minutes until tender and lightly charred, turning every so often so it cooks evenly.

7   Meanwhile, heat 6 tablespoons of rapeseed oil in a large frying pan over a medium-high heat. Add the first 2 chicken pieces and fry for a couple of minutes on each side until crispy and deeply golden. Transfer to a plate lined with paper towels while you fry the rest.

8   Once the broccoli is tender, transfer it into a bowl. Add your tamarind sauce, along with the crispy onion and garlic pieces. Season to taste with salt. Toss it around so all the pieces get coated.

9   Slice your crispy chicken pieces.

10   To serve, tong your broccoli onto plates with the sliced chicken and a dollop of curried yoghurt on the side, then sprinkle over the extra Bombay mix. Serve with lime wedges.

Spiced Tomatoey Chickpeas with Tzatziki

Serves
4

Cook time
1 hour

1 onion

1 carrot

2 celery sticks

400g tomato passata

200ml vegetable stock

1 tsp dried oregano

½ tsp dried mint

1 large posh jar of chickpeas,
or 2 × 400g tins

1 cinnamon stick

½ small bunch of fresh dill

For the tzatziki
½ cucumber

1 small garlic clove

1 tsp dried mint

200g thick natural yoghurt

juice of ½ lemon, *plus wedges
to serve*

salt, pepper and olive oil

The first time I went to Greece and ate gigantes beans, it blew my mind that what was essentially a baked bean could be so fragrant and glamorous. Flavouring legumes like this – with dried mint and cinnamon – is one of my all-time favourite ways to eat them, and I've swapped fat butter beans here for chickpeas. This can be prepped up to 3 days in advance, and is delicious eaten hot or at room temperature, making it an ideal lazy summer dinner on its own. Having said that, it uses mostly store-cupboard bits, so would also suit a winter's dinner. I often cook this as part of a larger spread, with grilled meats, flatbreads and earthy green filo pies.

1 Start by preparing the cucumber for your tzatziki. Grate the cucumber on a coarse grater, then pop it into a sieve set over a bowl. Add 1 teaspoon of salt and give it a good mix, then leave to sit for a bit. This will draw out the liquid from the cucumber.

2 Meanwhile, peel, halve and finely dice your onion. Finely dice your carrot and celery sticks too.

3 Heat a glug of olive oil in a large sauté pan over a medium heat. Add the onion, carrot and celery and cook for 10 minutes until everything has softened.

4 Add the passata and stock to the pan, along with the oregano and dried mint, then simmer for 5 minutes until slightly reduced.

5 Drain your chickpeas and give them a rinse, then pour them into the pan. Add the cinnamon stick and season with a little salt, then bring to a simmer. Cook gently for about 30 minutes, stirring occasionally to stop the mixture from sticking.

6 Meanwhile, return to your tzatziki. Squeeze the cucumber to remove any extra liquid, then tip it into a mixing bowl. Grate in the garlic, then add the dried mint, yoghurt and lemon juice. Mix, then season to taste with salt.

7 Pick the dill in small clusters.

8 Season your chickpeas to taste with salt. Spoon them into bowls, then top with dollops of tzatziki and a handful of dill. Serve with lemon wedges for squeezing.

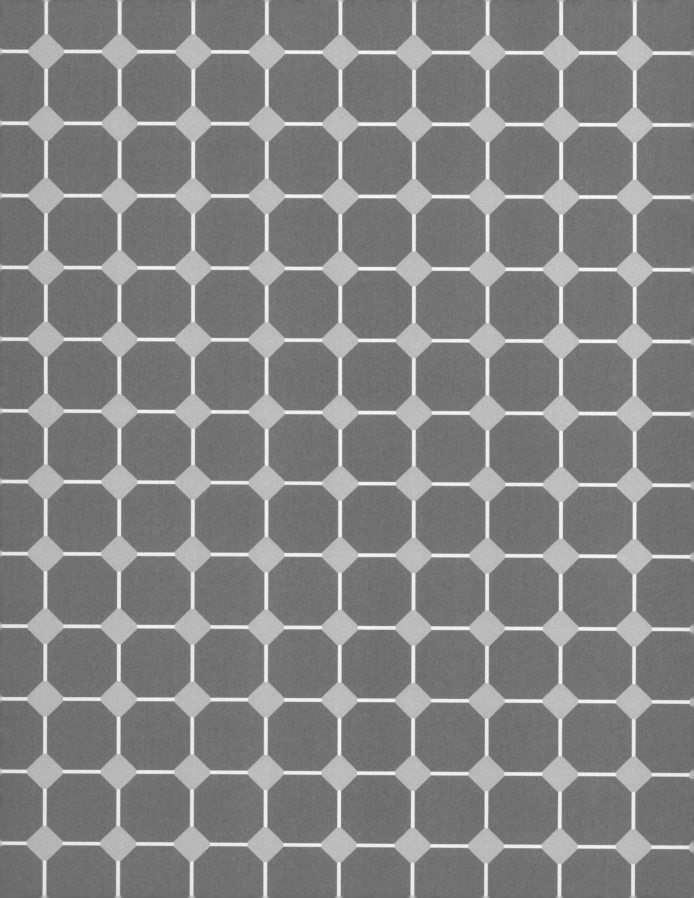

Pasta Party

It is a real challenge to choose my favourite carb. My brain automatically takes me to potatoes (how could I live without hash browns and crisps?), but I think the carb that I truly cook the most is pasta. This is why pasta gets its own chapter, and the other carbs are all bunched together (more on that later). Pasta is king, because you can throw together a ridiculously soothing plate of food in about 10 minutes. Equally, you can spend a leisurely afternoon making your own dough and simmering a ragu to create something fancier. It is a choice weapon for the lazy cook, but also the adventurous one. In this chapter, you'll find both – some recipes that are perfect for a midweek get-together, and others that are absolutely intended for a long Saturday cook, with the tunes blaring in the kitchen, and a nice bottle of red on the go.

Cheat's Sausage and Walnut Lasagne

Serves
4

Cook time
1 hour

100g walnuts

2 slices of white bread

700ml whole milk

75g Parmesan

2 shallots

3 garlic cloves

1 leek

½ small bunch of sage

6 good-quality pork sausages

¼ whole nutmeg

250g fresh lasagne sheets

125g mozzarella ball

20g butter

salt, pepper and olive oil

Some people may say this isn't a lasagne, but it uses lasagne sheets, so there you go. This is one of the first dishes that came to me when developing this book, and involves loads of ingredients that are a bit of me. Sausages! Leeks! Pasta! Creamy sauce! I wanted to give you a lasagne-ish for the days where you want the luxuriousness of a bubbly baked pasta, but don't have the time or energy to go through the faff of making a classic lasagne.

1   Place your walnuts in a cast-iron or shallow casserole dish and cover them with cold water. Bring to the boil, then simmer them gently for 5 minutes to soften.

2   Cut the crusts off your bread, then tear each slice into little pieces. Pop these into a medium-sized bowl, and pour over the milk. Leave to soak for 5 minutes.

3   Drain your walnuts, then place in a food processor. Use your hands to squeeze excess milk out of your bread over the bowl, reserving the milk, then add the squeezed bread to the food processor. Grate in 60g of the Parmesan, then pulse to a paste. Drizzle in the milk from the bowl, with the motor still running, to form a creamy sauce.

4   Peel and finely slice your shallots and garlic. Finely slice your leek and half the sage leaves.

5   Heat an ovenproof skillet or casserole dish over a medium heat. Squeeze the sausage meat out of its skins and fry for 5 minutes until golden and crispy. Remove from the pan with a slotted spoon, and set aside on a plate.

6   Add 2 tablespoons of olive oil to the pan, then tip in your shallots and leek. Cook for 15 minutes until they are totally soft, then add your garlic and sage, and cook for 2 minutes longer.

7   Return the sausage meat to the pan, then pour in your walnut sauce. Grate in the nutmeg, and season the sauce to taste with salt and pepper. Tear your lasagne sheets into pieces, then nestle these into the pan. Simmer for 3 minutes.

8   Preheat your grill to a high. Tear the mozzarella over the top of the mixture in the pan, then grate over the remaining 15g of Parmesan. Pop the pan under the grill for 5 minutes until bubbly.

9   Meanwhile, melt the butter in a frying pan over a medium heat, then add the remaining sage leaves. Fry for 2 minutes until the leaves are crispy and the butter is lightly browned.

10 Remove your pan from under the grill and drizzle over your sage and brown butter. Serve immediately.

Cavolo and Taleggio Pasta

Serves

4

Cook time
20 minutes

200g cavolo nero

2 garlic cloves

500g conchiglie, *or any other dried pasta shape you fancy*

250ml double cream

200ml whole milk

200g Taleggio

¼ whole nutmeg

30g Parmesan or vegetarian hard cheese, *plus 20g for sprinkling*

salt, pepper and olive oil

One of my earliest moments of hanger was cured by the meal that inspired this dish. On a family holiday to the Italian Alps, we struggled to find somewhere to eat after a long walk. After some time, we found a camping lodge. Although they did not sell food, they said they could rustle up some lunch for us, and proceeded to whip up a magical thing that I've thought of most weeks in the 20 years since. It was penne dressed simply in a cream, Taleggio and nutmeg sauce, and it was a revelation to my tiny ten-year-old mind. I've revamped this baby by injecting it with some bright green in the form of cavolo nero, in an attempt to give the indulgence a virtuous edge. Other greens would work in different seasons – spinach, chard or kale can be swapped in depending on what time of year it is.

1   Get a large saucepan of water on to boil. Salt it generously – it should be as seasoned as if it were a soup.

2   Tear your cavolo nero leaves off their stalks, then chop them into medium-sized pieces. Peel and finely chop the garlic.

3   Heat 2 tablespoons of olive oil in a sauté pan over a medium heat. Add the garlic and cook it gently for a minute until fragrant, then add the cavolo nero leaves. Add a splash of water to get some steam going, then gently cook for about 5 minutes.

4   Add your pasta to the saucepan of boiling water, and cook for a couple of minutes less than the packet instructions suggest, or until al dente.

5   Meanwhile, pour your cream and milk into the pan with the greens, and bring to a gentle simmer.

6   Chop your Taleggio, then add it to the pan with the creamy greens. Let it gently melt – this will thicken the sauce slightly.

7   Once your pasta is cooked, add a mugful of the pasta water to your sauce. Drain the pasta, then add this to the sauce as well. Give it a good mix, then grate in the nutmeg and 30g of the Parmesan. Season to taste with salt (your pasta water will have seasoned it already, so go gently), and about 15 twists of pepper.

8   Spoon the pasta into bowls, then top it with with a grating of your remaining Parmesan, and serve.

Hangover Pasta

Serves
4

Cook time
20 minutes

200g chorizo (*the softer ones are great, but if not a big ring will do*)

500g fusilli or radiatori

4 large garlic cloves

½ tsp chilli flakes

400g cherry tomatoes

2 tbsp tomato purée

200g mascarpone

50g Parmesan, *plus 20g for sprinkling*

½ small bunch of parsley

salt, pepper and olive oil

I have made a version of this dish somewhere in the realm of 347 times. When living with friends in my twenties, this was the meal I would cook us on a Saturday evening, after a Friday in all likelihood spent dancing along to the entirety of Beyoncé's Homecoming *in our pants in our living room, fuelled by tequila shots, or doing a marathon set of YouTube karaoke. I have fed this meal to a host of people with weary heads, who have dropped by for a debrief and a recovery evening watching* The Lord of the Rings*, and it always goes down a treat. It is also the only known cure to the Sunday scaries.*

1   Bring a large saucepan of water to a boil. Season it generously with salt, as though you were seasoning a soup.

2   Peel the skin off your chorizo and chop it into small chunks.

3   Heat 2 tablespoons of olive oil in a sauté pan over a medium heat. Add the chorizo and cook for 3 minutes, or until lots of the fat has rendered out.

4   Cook your pasta in the boiling water for a couple of minutes less than the packet instructions suggest, or until al dente.

5   Peel and finely slice the garlic, and add it to the chorizo pan, along with the chilli flakes. Cook gently for 1 minute.

6   Add the cherry tomatoes and tomato purée to the pan and cook for 5 minutes, pressing down on the tomatoes to release their juices and create a thick sauce.

7   Stir in the mascarpone until it has fully melted, then grate in the Parmesan. Roughly chop your parsley and sprinkle that in, too. Season to taste with salt and 15 twists of black pepper.

8   Drain the pasta, reserving a mugful of the pasta cooking water. Tip the pasta into the sauce, adding splashes of the cooking water to help it all come together as a silky sauce that clings to the pasta.

9   Spoon your pasta onto plates, then top with a little more grated Parmesan to serve.

Chicken Butter, Pancetta and Leek Tagliatelle

Serves
2

Cook time
30 minutes

6 sage leaves

10g panko breadcrumbs

40g butter

1 garlic clove

½ leek

70g diced pancetta

4 thyme sprigs

450ml good-quality
chicken stock

250g dried egg tagliatelle

3 tbsp double cream

salt, pepper and olive oil

Butter has to be in my top five foodstuffs of all time. Fat carries flavour, and when that fat is butter, it carries any dish on a magic carpet ride to a very beautiful place. All meals are made better for it. I use butter here to emulsify chicken stock, to thicken it into a particularly sexy pasta sauce. It tastes a bit like a roast dinner, which I'm not sure can ever be a bad thing. When I say good-quality stock, I mean homemade, or the fancy sort you get in liquid form in the supermarket. A cube here would make your finished dish far too salty, so avoid this at all costs.

1 Bring a large saucepan of water to the boil. Season it to taste with salt, as though it were a soup you are about to eat.

2 Finely slice your sage leaves. Heat 2 tablespoons of olive oil in a medium-sized frying pan over a medium heat. Add the sage and breadcrumbs and toast them for 3 minutes, stirring frequently, until the crumbs have turned a light golden brown. Season with ½ teaspoon of salt, then set aside.

3 Dice the butter into small cubes. Peel and finely chop the garlic. Finely slice the leek.

4 Heat 1 tablespoon of olive oil in a medium-sized sauté pan over a medium heat. Add the pancetta, and fry it until it's crispy and the fat has rendered out. Remove from the pan with a slotted spoon.

5 Reduce the heat to low, then add your leek to the pan and gently cook it in the pancetta fat for 5 minutes until softened. Add the garlic and thyme, and cook for another minute until fragrant. Now pour in the chicken stock, and bring it to a gentle simmer. Cook for about 8 minutes until reduced by about two-thirds.

6 Meanwhile, drop your tagliatelle into the boiling water and cook it for 3–4 minutes, or until it is just tender.

7 Once your stock has reduced, add the butter, a cube at a time, whisking each time until the cube has melted before adding another. Over time, the butter will emulsify with the stock, and thicken into a thick, glossy sauce. Stir in the double cream.

8 Tong your tagliatelle directly into the sauce, and add a splash of its cooking water to loosen. Return the pancetta to the pan, then give it all a really good mix to bring everything together. Season with about 10 twists of black pepper (it shouldn't need any more salt, but you could add more if you like) and sprinkle over the herby breadcrumbs, then tong it on to plates and serve.

Squash, Anchovy and Mascarpone Pasta

Serves
4

Cook time
50 minutes

1 small butternut squash

1 onion

3 garlic cloves

500g rigatoni

2 tbsp tomato purée

50g tin of anchovy fillets

½ tsp chilli flakes

150g mascarpone

40g Parmesan, *plus 20g for sprinkling*

½ small bunch of sage

30g butter

salt, pepper and olive oil

There are a few ingredients that, when you start to enjoy them, signify the start of adulthood to me. Capers, dill and marmalade all fall into this category, and so do anchovies. Intensely fishy and salty, only the most sophisticated of children enjoy them, but all sophisticated adults do. This sauce is packed with them, and it is classy as hell. The sweetness of squash and creamy mascarpone temper the bossiness of an anchovy, making for a very harmonious sauce. Cook this up for friends who appreciate a bit of oomph on a midweek evening, and I assure you they will leave very happy.

1 Preheat your oven to 230°C/210°C fan/gas mark 8.

2 Peel your squash and remove the seeds, then cut the flesh into chunks. Tip into a roasting tray and drizzle over 1 tablespoon of olive oil. Season with salt, then roast for 30 minutes until the squash chunks are caramelised and tender.

3 Meanwhile, peel and finely chop your onion and garlic.

4 Heat 4 tablespoons of olive oil in a sauté pan over a medium-low heat. Add your onion and cook for 20 minutes until totally soft.

5 Bring a large saucepan of water to the boil. Season it generously with salt, as though it were a soup you were about to eat. Tip your rigatoni into the boiling water, and cook it for a few minutes less than the packet instructions suggest, or until al dente.

6 Add the tomato purée to your onions, and cook for 5 minutes until the mixture has darkened. Add the drained anchovies, garlic and chilli flakes to the pan and cook for 2 minutes more, squashing down the anchovies with your spoon so they form a paste.

7 Add the roasted squash to the pan and mash it down with your spoon to make a rustic purée. Stir in the mascarpone; it will melt down and meld with your other ingredients to make a sauce.

8 Spoon your pasta directly into the sauce with a slotted spoon, along with a ladleful of the pasta water. Grate in 40g Parmesan, and give it all a good mix to form a glossy sauce, adding more pasta water if you need. Season to taste with salt and 10 twists of black pepper.

9 Pick the leaves off your sage. Melt the butter in a small frying pan over a medium heat. Add your sage leaves and fry for about 30 seconds, or until they have darkened in colour and crisped up.

10 Spoon your pasta onto plates, then top with your crispy sage leaves and butter. Sprinkle over the remaining Parmesan and serve.

Chestnut and Mushroom Rotolo

Serves

4

Cook time
1 hour 45 minutes,
plus soaking and resting

15g dried porcini mushrooms

1 onion

1 leek

85g butter

900g chestnut mushrooms

3 garlic cloves

½ small bunch of sage

180g cooked chestnuts

1 tbsp tomato purée

200g tinned chopped tomatoes

60g plain flour

900ml whole milk

75g Parmesan or vegetarian
hard cheese

½ whole nutmeg

125g mozzarella ball

a few thyme leaves, *to serve*

For the pasta
300g '00' flour

3 eggs

30g fine semolina, *for dusting*

salt, pepper and olive oil

Tip
*Use shop-bought lasagne sheets
if you are short on time.*

This is one of the most beautiful dishes in this book, I think. It is, admittedly, a bit of a fiddly one, but it's a fun way to spend a leisurely afternoon, and you do get a really quite lovely bowl of pasta at the end of it, so I reckon it is worth it. The ragu is a wintery mix of mushrooms, chestnuts and sage, making it feel pretty festive; it's the kind of dinner you'd like to demolish after a wintry walk, with the fire crackling in the background. It can all be assembled up to a day in advance, or even frozen pre-bake, so you can throw it all together when you have time and enjoy it another day.

1   Tip your dried porcini mushrooms into a mug, then pour over 200ml boiling water. Leave to soak for 20 minutes.

2   Peel and finely chop your onion, and finely slice your leek.

3   Melt 25g of the butter in a large casserole dish over a medium heat. Add the onion and leek, and cook them gently for about 15 minutes until totally softened.

4   When the mushrooms have soaked for 20 minutes, lift them out of the liquid, reserving the rich mushroom stock. In a food processor, pulse your chestnut and porcini mushrooms in batches to break them up into a fine mince. Heat 1 tablespoon of olive oil in a large frying pan over a high heat. Add half your minced mushrooms to the pan, and fry for about 7 minutes until they have totally reduced and started to caramelise. Transfer to a plate and repeat with the remaining mushrooms.

5   Peel and finely chop your garlic. Finely chop your sage. Pulse your chestnuts in the food processor to break them up into little pieces.

6   Once the onion and leek are cooked, add the garlic and sage to the pan, along with the tomato purée. Cook for 2 minutes, then add the minced mushrooms and chestnuts, along with your porcini mushroom liquid and the tinned tomatoes. Stir and simmer for 5 minutes, then season to taste with salt and 15 twists of black pepper. Take off the heat and allow to cool to room temperature.

7   To make your pasta dough, pour your '00' flour into a clean food processor, and crack in your eggs. Whizz together until you have a clumpy dough. Tip this out onto your work surface dusted with fine semolina, and give it a good knead until it has come together as a smooth dough. Wrap it in cling film, and leave to rest at room temperature for 20 minutes.

continues overleaf

Chestnut and Mushroom Rotolo

8 Preheat your oven to 210°C/190°C fan/gas mark 6½.

9 Melt the remaining 60g of butter in a medium-sized saucepan over a medium heat. Add the plain flour and cook it out for 2 minutes, then gradually pour in your milk in small increments, whisking to fully incorporate between additions, until you have a smooth sauce.

10 Bring your sauce to the boil, then reduce the heat to a simmer. Grate in 60g of your Parmesan and the nutmeg. Season to taste with salt and pepper.

11 Take 6 tablespoons of this sauce and spoon it into your mushroom mixture. Pour the remaining sauce into a large, wide baking dish – I like using a shallow 30cm casserole dish.

12 Bring a large pan of water to the boil, and salt it generously.

13 Dust your work surface with semolina. Cut your pasta dough into 4 equal-sized pieces. Take the first piece, wrapping the rest in cling film, and use a pasta roller on the second-thinnest setting to roll out the dough. Cut this piece of dough in half horizontally, then repeat with the rest of the pasta dough.

14 Cook each piece of pasta for a minute in the boiling water, then carefully lift out of the pan and lay on a large baking tray.

15 Divide the mushroom filling between the pieces of pasta, and spread it all over the surface. Roll up each one so you have 8 long mushroom-filled sausage shapes. Cut these sausages into 2.5cm lengths.

16 Nestle each pasta shape into your sauce, arranging them on their ends so you can see their swirly inside pattern. You can push them down a little so they stand up sturdily. Once all your pasta is in the dish, tear over the mozzarella and sprinkle over the remaining Parmesan. Bake for 25 minutes.

17 To serve, sprinkle over some thyme, and dig in.

Courgette Pasta e Ceci

Serves
4

Cook time
1 hour

1 small onion

2 celery sticks

3 garlic cloves

3 courgettes

6 thyme sprigs

15g pine nuts

20g basil

400g tin of chickpeas

1 litre vegetable stock

200g ditalini *(or macaroni or orzo if you can't find ditalini)*

zest and juice of 1 lemon

salt, pepper and olive oil

Pasta e ceci is a perfect example of a humble, hearty, inexpensive meal that tastes so much better than some meals made with ingredients three times the price. Chickpeas and pasta together create a creamy, starchy base that is somewhere between a soup and a stew, ideal for providing comfort on chillier summer days. Traditionally, the base is a sofrito tinged red with tomato, but I wanted to make a version that felt greener and fresher, so I've roped in courgettes to help. The pesto drizzle is essential to bring a bit of brightness into a dish that could otherwise feel quite heavy.

1   Peel and finely chop your onion. Finely chop your celery.

2   Heat 4 tablespoons of olive oil in a saucepan over a medium-low heat. Add the onion and celery and a good pinch of salt, then sweat it down for about 10 minutes until the mixture is totally softened.

3   Meanwhile, peel and finely chop your garlic. Finely slice your courgettes.

4   Once the onion and celery mixture is soft, add three-quarters of your garlic. Cook it out for a minute, then tip your courgettes into the pan. Pick in the thyme leaves, then turn the heat right down. Cook for about 15 minutes, stirring occasionally so that everything cooks evenly.

5   Meanwhile, make your pesto. Toast your pine nuts in a dry frying pan over a medium heat for 5 minutes, then set aside to cool slightly. Bash your remaining garlic to a paste using a pestle and mortar. Add the basil leaves and bash again, then add the toasted pine nuts and bash once more. Add 4 tablespoons of olive oil, and give it all a mix to combine. Season to taste with salt.

6   Drain your chickpeas and give them a rinse. Add them to the pan with the vegetables, then pour in the veg stock. Simmer for 5 minutes.

7   Ladle half of your veg and chickpea mixture (along with half of the liquid) into a blender, and whizz to a smooth consistency. Pour this back into the pan.

8   Season your sauce to taste with salt and 15 twists of black pepper, then bring the mixture back to a simmer. Add your ditalini and cook for about 8 minutes, or until the pasta is just al dente. Stir frequently so it doesn't stick to the bottom, and add occasional splashes of water if your pasta is being particularly thirsty.

9   Zest in the lemon, then squeeze in all the juice. Adjust the seasoning if you need. Spoon it into bowls, and dollop some pesto in the middle to serve.

Chicken and Ricotta Meatballs with Green Spaghetti

Serves
4

Cook time
35 minutes, plus resting

400g skinless chicken thigh fillets

zest and juice of ½ lemon

250g ricotta

½ small bunch of parsley

70g fresh white breadcrumbs

80g Parmesan, *plus 20g for sprinkling*

100g watercress

small bunch of basil

50g sunflower seeds

1 garlic clove

400g spaghetti

salt, pepper and olive oil

Red sauce has dominated the meatball market for too long, and I say enough's enough. Okay, I also love the classic tomato sauce and polpette combo, but there is something lighter and fresher about this version that I sometimes prefer. The leanness of chicken mince enriched with milky ricotta and Parmesan creates an impossibly tender little thing to stab with your fork and twirl around in a silky green spaghetti skirt. Maybe you'll twirl around the kitchen a little, you'll like it that much. The meatballs can be prepared a day in advance, so you can whip this up in no time.

1 Chop your chicken thigh fillets into pieces, then add these to a food processor. Add the lemon zest and 120g of the ricotta, as well as 1 teaspoon of salt and 15 twists of black pepper. Pulse until you have a smooth paste. Grate in 30g of your Parmesan, then finely chop your parsley and add this too, as well as your breadcrumbs. Give it a stir so it's all combined.

2 Roll your mixture into 12 even-sized balls. Pop these on a tray, and place them in the fridge for 15 minutes to firm up.

3 Meanwhile, give your food processor a clean, then move on to making your pesto. In the food processor, combine the watercress, basil, sunflower seeds, peeled garlic clove and remaining 50g of Parmesan. Whizz it up to form a smooth green paste, then drizzle in 50ml of olive oil so that you have a smooth sauce. Add the lemon juice and the remaining ricotta, pulse the machine briefly, then season to taste with salt.

4 Bring a large saucepan filled with water to the boil, and season it with salt as though it were a soup you were about to eat.

5 Heat 2 tablespoons of olive oil in a large sauté pan over a medium heat. Add your meatballs to the pan and cook for about 10 minutes, turning them frequently so that they cook evenly and take on some colour on the outside.

6 Meanwhile, add your spaghetti to the pan of boiling water. Cook your pasta for a couple of minutes less than the packet instructions require, or until it is just al dente.

7 Once it's cooked, tong your spaghetti directly into the meatball pan, along with a ladleful of the pasta cooking water. Add your pesto to the pan, and give it a good toss so that each strand of spaghetti is coated in the green sauce. Add as much pasta water as you need to get the sauce glossy. Adjust the seasoning if needed.

8 Divide the spaghetti and meatballs between plates, and serve it up with a little extra Parmesan.

(Almost) No-Cook Tomato and Ricotta Pasta

Serves
4

Cook time
20 minutes, plus resting

300g tomatoes

1 small garlic clove

zest of 1 lemon and juice of ½

500g casarecce *(or penne if you can't find casarecce)*

250g ricotta

small bunch of dill

50g Parmesan or vegetarian hard cheese

salt, pepper and olive oil

I am not someone who handles heat well. In the London summer infernos of recent years, I have developed a coping mechanism that involves sprawling out on the sofa with a multitude of fans angled towards me, switching intermittently between dramatically howling and sucking on an ice lolly for comfort. I will, wherever possible, dodge long spells spent near the hobs, only choosing to grace them with my presence when I can cook a rapid meal that tastes so fresh that I forget how uncomfortable I am. This meal is that very self-soothing thing. The only heat used is to simmer the casarecce, and then you can retreat back to your perch with a cooling bowl of pasta tossed with silky, lemony ricotta, marinated tomatoes and lots of dill. It's a creamy pasta salad, but with no mayonnaise in sight. I developed this recipe while working at Mob during a particularly sweltering summer, and it is now a heatwave staple for me.

1 Cut your tomatoes into chunks, then add them to a bowl. Grate in your garlic clove and lemon zest, then add the lemon juice, along with 2 tablespoons of olive oil and a pinch of salt. Stir, then leave to sit at room temperature – you could do this a few hours in advance, if you like.

2 Bring a large saucepan of water to the boil. Salt it well. Tip your pasta into the pan and and cook it for a few minutes less than the packet instructions suggest, or until it is just al dente.

3 Meanwhile, finely chop your dill.

4 In a large bowl, combine your ricotta with 4 tablespoons of olive oil, then grate in the Parmesan. Give it a good whisk until it is totally smooth.

5 When your pasta is cooked, add a ladleful of your pasta water to the ricotta mixture, and whisk until it comes together smoothly.

6 Drain your pasta, then tip it into the ricotta mixture. Add the tomatoes and most of the chopped dill, and give it all a good stir.

7 Spoon into bowls and finish with some more fresh dill and some black pepper. Serve it up.

Smoked Almond and Confit Tomato Mafaldine

Serves
6

Cook time
1 hour 20 minutes

8 garlic cloves

4 × 400g tins of whole plum tomatoes

1 tsp chilli flakes

75g smoked almonds

600g mafaldine (*or spaghetti if you can't find mafaldine*)

½ small bunch of basil

salt, pepper and olive oil

Everyone has their own version of a simple tomato pasta, a meal that is so beloved by many. There are a few variations I make. I love the Marcella Hazan method of simmering it gently with half an onion and a big knob of butter. I also love slow-roasting big, beefy tomatoes, then mashing them to form something concentrated and jammy. The method I use here is inspired by the one served at South London stalwart Forza Wine, where those clever dudes roast whole tinned plum tomatoes to get a good char on them, then enrich it with butter to form a sauce that sees people booking tables in advance. I've taken this method and gone somewhere a little different with it; I wanted it to have plant-based creaminess and depth, so I've whizzed it up with smoked almonds, and it works a charm.

1   Preheat your oven to 230°C/210°C fan/gas mark 8.

2   Peel your garlic cloves, then finely slice them. Pour your tinned tomatoes into a colander, and rinse off the tomato juice.

3   Tip the tomatoes into a small baking dish, then scatter the chilli flakes and garlic on top. Pour over 8 tablespoons of olive oil – you basically want the tomatoes to confit – then place the tray in the oven. Cook for 30 minutes.

4   Meanwhile, tip the almonds into a heatproof bowl, then pour over 100ml boiling water to cover them. Leave to soak while the tomatoes are roasting.

5   After the 30 minutes are up, remove your tomatoes from the oven and stir to mix them up a bit. Return to the oven for another 30 minutes – they should get a nice char on them.

6   Bring a saucepan of water to the boil, and salt it as though it were a soup. Add your mafaldine, and cook it for a couple of minutes less than the packet instructions suggest, or until al dente.

7   Tip your almonds, along with their water, into a blender, then whizz them up to combine. Add your tomatoes to the blender, then whizz them up to form a creamy sauce.

8   Pour this sauce into a sauté pan over a medium-low heat, and bring it to a simmer. Once your pasta is cooked, add a ladleful of pasta water to the pan, then tong in the pasta. Mix until you have a glossy sauce that totally coats your pasta, adding more pasta water if needed. Season to taste with salt and pepper – your pasta water will have seasoned it a little already, so go gently. Pick the leaves off your basil, and stir these through, too.

9   Tong the pasta into bowls, finish with some black pepper and serve.

Pulled Oyster Mushroom Ragu

Serves
8

Cook time
1 hour 40 minutes,
plus soaking

30g dried porcini mushrooms

2 large onions

4 garlic cloves

2 carrots

4 celery sticks

½ small bunch of rosemary

½ small bunch of thyme

1kg king oyster mushrooms

3 tbsp dark soy sauce

4 tbsp tomato purée

300ml red wine

2 × 400g tins of whole
plum tomatoes

2 tbsp yeast extract
(I use Marmite)

1 bay leaf

30g panko breadcrumbs

400g rigatoni or paccheri

¼ small bunch of parsley

salt, pepper and olive oil

A king oyster mushroom is a valuable chameleon when it comes to plant-based cooking. By prepping it in different ways, you can give it all kinds of textures and flavours, making it carnitas-like, chicken-like, crispy duck-like, or in this case, beef shin-like. This is the meatiest ragu I've ever made without any meat. You can also batch-cook and freeze it, much like a meaty ragu. I suggest using rigatoni or paccheri here – as photographer Lizzie Mayson said, 'Once you go paccheri, you don't go baccheri.'

1. Pop your porcini mushrooms into a heatproof jug and pour over 600ml boiling water. Leave to soak for 20 minutes, then remove the mushrooms from the liquid (keep the liquid) and finely chop them.

2. Peel and finely chop your onions and garlic. Finely chop your carrots, celery, rosemary and thyme. Tear the oyster mushrooms into fine strips.

3. Heat 1 tablespoon of olive oil in a large frying pan over a high heat. Add the oyster mushrooms, and cook for 10 minutes until reduced and slightly caramelised. Add your dark soy sauce and keep cooking until the sauce reduces down, then set aside until later.

4. Heat 8 tablespoons of olive oil in a cast-iron pot over a medium heat. Add your onions, carrots and celery, then reduce the heat to low-medium and fry gently for 15 minutes until softened. Now tip in your tomato purée and garlic, along with all but ½ teaspoon each of your rosemary and thyme, and cook for another 2 minutes.

5. Pour your wine into the pan and stir until it has reduced by three-quarters. Add the tomatoes, porcini mushroom stock, chopped porcini, shredded oyster mushrooms, yeast extract and bay leaf. Give it a good mix and bring the mixture to the boil, then reduce the heat to low and simmer for an hour.

6. Heat 5 tablespoons of olive oil in a frying pan over a medium heat. Add the breadcrumbs and remaining rosemary and thyme, season to taste with salt, and give it all a stir. Toast for about 5 minutes until you have crisp, golden breadcrumbs. They go quickly, so keep an eye out. Finely chop your parsley, and set aside.

7. Cook your pasta in a large saucepan of salted water for a couple of minutes less than the packet instructions suggest, or until al dente. Drain, reserving a mugful of the water.

8. Season to taste with salt and about 15 twists of black pepper, then toss in your pasta, along with the reserved pasta water. Mix until your sauce coats the pasta, adding more pasta water if needed.

9. Serve in bowls, topped with your crispy breadcrumbs and parsley.

Crabby Cavatelli

Serves
4

Cook time
1 hour, plus resting

pinch of saffron
(optional)

400g fine semolina,
plus 50g for sprinkling

1 tsp chilli flakes

50g panko breadcrumbs

zest and juice of 1 lemon

4 garlic cloves

400g cherry tomatoes

2 tbsp tomato purée

150ml white wine

200g white crab meat

100g brown crab meat

small bunch of parsley

1 tbsp crème fraîche

salt, pepper and olive oil

Crab feels like one of the most fabulous ingredients you can serve up. The white meat is clean, sweet and meaty, while the brown is umami-rich and decadent. Using a combo of the two gives you an absolute saucepot of a pasta dish that will make anyone eating it feel like a rockstar. Making pasta for people is one of my love languages, and cavatelli is great shape because you don't even need a pasta roller. The saffron is not essential, but it gives the pasta a lovely sunshine-yellow hue. If you aren't using it, just start with lukewarm water.

1   If you're using saffron, place it in a heatproof jug, then pour over 200ml boiling water. Set aside and allow to cool to room temperature.

2   Tip 400g of your semolina onto a clean work surface, and make a large well in the middle. Pour your room-temperature saffron water into the well (or just use lukewarm water), then gradually flick in some of the semolina, mixing it with a knife to form a paste. Gradually incorporate more semolina, being careful not to breach the semolina 'walls' until you have a thicker paste in the centre. Gradually flick in all of the semolina until you have a stiff dough.

3   Knead your dough for about 5 minutes until it is really smooth and tacky, then wrap it in cling film and leave it to rest for 20 minutes.

4   Meanwhile, make your chilli breadcrumbs. Heat 3 tablespoons of olive oil in a frying pan over a medium heat. Add ½ teaspoon of the chilli flakes, along with the breadcrumbs. Toast for a few minutes until golden, then tip them into a bowl to stop them from cooking any longer. Grate in the lemon zest and season to taste with salt, then give it a mix. Set aside until later.

5   Once your dough has rested, unwrap it and divide into 4 portions. Rewrap 3 of the portions in cling film, then roll the other dough piece into a long worm shape about 2cm wide. Chop this worm into 2cm chunks.

6   Take a gnocchi board, or the back of a fork, and place a piece of dough on it. Push your dough forwards with the side of your thumb to curl it up into a small shell shape, patterned with the lines of the board or fork. This is your cavatelli. Repeat with all the remaining dough sections, until you have lots of little pasta shapes. Sprinkle a large baking tray with your remaining semolina, and place the cavatelli inside. You can do this up to 8 hours in advance.

7   Now let's move on to your crabby sauce. Peel and finely slice the garlic, and halve the cherry tomatoes.

continues overleaf

8   Pour 4 tablespoons of olive oil into a sauté pan over a medium heat, and add the sliced garlic while the pan is still warming up. Let it sizzle for a couple of minutes until it is fragrant and just starting to colour a little.

9   Tip in your cherry tomatoes and the remaining ½ teaspoon of chilli flakes, and let these cook for about 5 minutes. Squish the cherry tomatoes down with the back of your spoon so they start to break down and get saucy. Add your tomato purée and cook for 5 minutes until the mixture has darkened slightly and is starting to get a bit stuck on the base of your pan. Pour in the wine, and cook for 3 minutes to let it reduce by half.

10 Get your white and brown crab meat in there and give it all a good mix, then simmer gently for 10 minutes.

11 Bring a large saucepan of water to the boil, and season it with salt as if it were a soup you are about to eat. Tip in your cavatelli, and simmer for 4 minutes.

12 Meanwhile, finely chop your parsley, and tip this into the pan with the crab. Spoon in the crème fraîche and squeeze in the lemon juice, then season it to taste with salt and 10 twists of black pepper. Add a ladleful of your pasta water, then lift your cooked pasta into the sauce with a slotted spoon. Give it a mix so that each piece of pasta is totally coated in sauce, adding more pasta water if you need to make it juicy.

13 Spoon your pasta into bowls and sprinkle over your breadcrumbs, then serve.

Piggy Porcini Lasagne

Serves
8

Cook time
5 hours (mostly hands-off)

1 onion

2 celery sticks

160g pancetta

30g porcini mushrooms

1kg pork shoulder chunks

2 garlic cloves

2 tbsp tomato purée

150ml white wine

400g tinned chopped tomatoes

150ml chicken stock

1 rosemary sprig

70g butter

70g plain flour

975ml milk

60g Parmesan

100g mozzarella

16 dried lasagne sheets

salt, pepper and olive oil

It would feel really wrong to write a book without including a lasagne, arguably the finest dish ever to be created, and probably my number one food when it comes to feeding a crowd. This ragu is a grown-up, autumnal mega babe – all sweet, salty pork, with some deep, earthy porcini to give it oomph. A labour of love, but oh so worth it. I once did a pop-up at The Hoxton in Southwark, where I served up ludicrously big wedges of a version of this bad boy as the main, and it went down an absolute treat. When I was testing it, my cat Slinky ate the entire top layer when I left the room, so it has her seal of approval, too. You could do it with pig cheeks or leg chunks instead of shoulder, if those float your boat.

1   Preheat your oven to 160°C/140°C fan/gas mark 3.

2   Peel and finely chop your onion. Finely chop your celery.

3   Heat 2 tablespoons of olive oil in a casserole dish over a low heat. Add your pancetta and fry until crisp, then remove and set aside on a plate. Add the onion and celery to the casserole dish and cook for 20 minutes, until it has totally softened and taken on a bit of colour.

4   While your onion cooks, tip your dried porcini mushrooms into a heatproof bowl or mug and pour over 200ml boiling water. Leave to soak.

5   Heat 1 teaspoon of olive oil in a frying pan over a high heat. Add a third of the pork chunks and fry for a minute or two on each side to brown them, then remove and set aside on a plate. Deglaze the pan with water and repeat with the remaining pork, saving those porky juices.

6   Peel and finely chop your garlic.

7   Add the tomato purée to the veg pan, and cook for 5 minutes until the mixture gets dark and sticks to the base of the pan. Stir in the garlic and cook for 2 minutes, then pour in the white wine and cook for 3 minutes to reduce it right down.

8   Remove your porcini mushrooms from their liquid and finely chop them. Make sure you save the soaking liquid – it is gold dust.

9   Tip the pork chunks and pancetta into the casserole dish, along with your tinned tomatoes, chopped porcini mushrooms, chicken stock, porcini stock, any porky juices and your rosemary sprig. Bring the mixture to a simmer, then cover it with a lid, and place the pan in the oven for 3½ hours.

continues overleaf

Piggy Porcini Lasagne

10 Remove your dish from the oven and increase the oven temperature to 220°C/200°C fan/gas mark 7.

11 Remove your rosemary sprig from the casserole dish, then use two forks to shred the meat; it should easily fall apart. Place the casserole dish over a medium heat and cook for 5–10 minutes, or until the sauce coats the back of a spoon. Season to taste with salt and 15 twists of black pepper – your pancetta will have seasoned it a little already, so go gently.

12 To make the white sauce, melt your butter in a large saucepan over a medium-low heat. Add the flour and cook it out for 2 minutes. Gradually pour in the milk in small increments, stirring all the while and ensuring each addition is incorporated in a smooth paste before adding more.

13 Once all the milk has been added, bring the mixture to the boil and let it simmer for 3 minutes. This will thicken it.

14 Remove the pan from the heat, then add 50g of your Parmesan and all of your mozzarella. Stir to combine and melt the cheeses, then season to taste with salt and 15 twists of black pepper.

15 Pour a little of the white sauce into the base of a 32 × 25cm baking dish, followed by a little of the ragu. Arrange a layer of lasagne sheets neatly on top, snapping sheets where necessary to plug the gaps. Pour over a quarter of your remaining ragu, followed by a quarter of your remaining white sauce, then more lasagne sheets. Continue like this until you are out of all your mixtures.

16 Finish with a layer of ragu and white sauce, pushing it all the way to the edges so the lasagne sheets are totally covered. Sprinkle with the remaining Parmesan, then bake it for 45 minutes until bubbly and oozing.

17 Let your lasagne stand for 5–10 minutes before carving it into slices and serving.

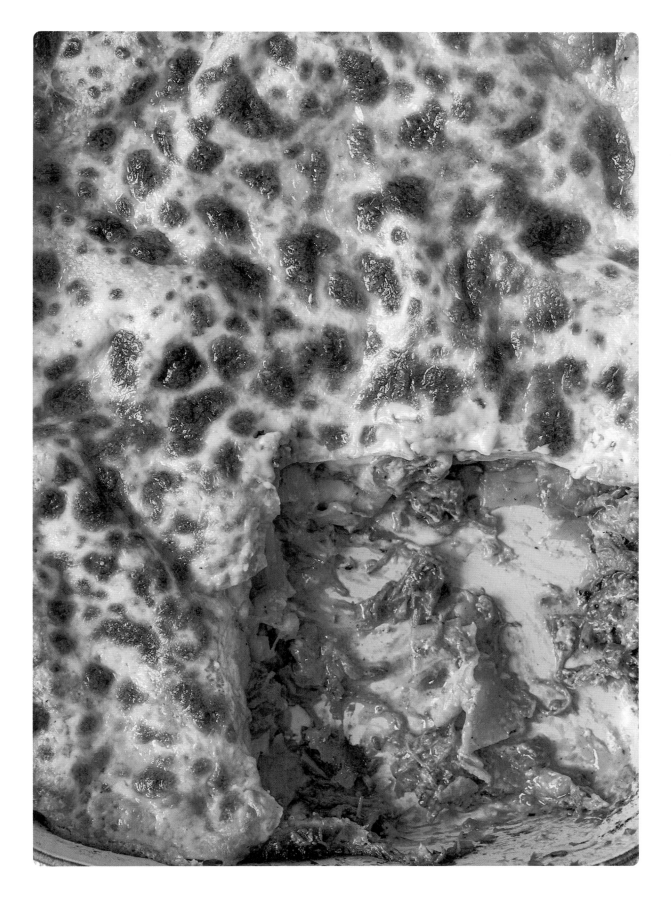

Chipotle Vodka Gnocchi Bake

Serves
4

Cook time
30 minutes

1 red onion

2 garlic cloves

100g Parmesan or vegetarian
hard cheese

2 tbsp chipotle chilli paste

150g tomato purée

50ml vodka

100g sour cream

75ml double cream

500g shop-bought gnocchi

a few basil leaves

125g mozzarella ball

salt, pepper and olive oil

Vodka pasta has become something of an internet sensation in the last few years, and understandably so. Pretty orange hues and indulgent, creamy textures make for a very Instagrammable thing, so big steaming bowls of the stuff being wheeled out of New York Italian eateries break the internet on a regular basis. The flavours are rich but simple – darkened tomato purée for savouriness, cream for silkiness, a bit of chilli heat. I add an extra layer of smokiness here by swapping out chilli flakes for chipotle chilli paste, and I also add the tang of sour cream. Not traditional in any sense, but it is rather lovely, nonetheless.

1   Peel and finely chop your onion and garlic. Grate your Parmesan.

2   Heat 3 tablespoons of olive oil in a sauté pan over a medium heat. Tip in your onion and fry for 15 minutes until it is totally soft, adding occasional splashes of water to stop it from sticking and to speed along the cooking time.

3   Add your garlic, then cook it out for a minute. Spoon in your chipotle chilli paste and tomato purée, then cook them both for about 5 minutes. It should get nice and dark, and begin sticking to the bottom of your pan.

4   Preheat your grill to high.

5   Pour the vodka into the pan and scrape the base of the pan to deglaze, then add the sour cream and double cream. Give it all a mix, and reduce the heat to low. Add enough water to make a smooth, silky, loose sauce.

6   Bring a large pan of salted water to the boil, then tip in your gnocchi. Cook for about 2 minutes until they rise to the surface.

7   Lift your gnocchi into the pan of sauce using a slotted spoon, then add 75g of your Parmesan cheese and a splash of the gnocchi cooking water to loosen it up. Season to taste with salt – the gnocchi water will have seasoned it a bit already, so go gently.

8   Tip the mixture into a 30 × 25cm baking dish, then scatter over most of the basil and tear over your mozzarella. Sprinkle over your remaining Parmesan, then pop the dish under the grill. Grill for about 5 minutes until the top is bubbly and golden.

9   Sprinkle the remaining fresh basil leaves over the top, then serve in bowls.

Lamb Neck and Olive Orzo

Serves
6

Cook time
2 hours 30 minutes

1 red onion

3 garlic cloves

2 celery sticks

1 rosemary sprig

750g lamb neck fillets

2 tbsp tomato purée

1 tsp dried oregano

150ml white wine

150g pitted kalamata olives

400g passata

900ml chicken stock

1 cinnamon stick

350g orzo

1 lemon

½ small bunch of parsley

salt, pepper and olive oil

Ordering in restaurants can be a perilous activity. I have several memories of spending good chunks of a meal staring longingly at what the person sitting next to me was eating, wishing I'd ordered the same. Luckily, we now live in the era of sharing plates, so this situation occurs less, but I have a distinct memory from a trip to Crete in 2010 where such a thing did happen. I couldn't even tell you what I ordered, but my mum had a youvetsi – a beef stew humming with cinnamon, with orzo baked into it. Thankfully, she is a selfless woman, and let bratty teenage me eat a good chunk of it. That was the inspiration for this dish, here made with lamb instead of beef, studded with kalamata olives for extra oomph.

1   Preheat your oven to 180°C/160°C fan/gas mark 4.

2   Peel and finely chop your onion and garlic. Finely chop your celery and rosemary leaves.

3   Heat 2 tablespoons of olive oil in a frying pan over a high heat. Cut your lamb neck into large chunks about 5cm big, and season them with a teaspoon of salt. Working in batches, add the chunks to the frying pan, searing on each side for a minute or two until you get a deep golden colour. Remove the pieces from the pan and set aside on a plate, then repeat with the remaining meat.

4   Heat 5 tablespoons of olive oil in a large casserole dish over a medium heat. Tip in your onion and celery, then cook gently for 15 minutes until it is all soft. Add your tomato purée, dried oregano and chopped rosemary, along with two-thirds of your chopped garlic, and cook for 5 minutes until the tomato purée darkens.

5   Pour in the wine, then cook for 3 minutes to let the wine reduce by half. Add your lamb to the casserole dish, along with the kalamata olives, then pour in the passata and chicken stock. Bring the mixture up to a simmer, then drop in the cinnamon stick. Season with ½ teaspoon of salt, then cover with a lid and pop in the oven for 1 hour and 30 minutes.

6   Remove from the oven and check the seasoning of the sauce. Tip in the orzo and give it a good mix, then return to the oven, uncovered, to bake for 15 minutes.

7   Meanwhile, make a quick little gremolata. Peel the rind off your lemon, then carefully remove any chunky bits of white pith. Very finely slice the rind, and then dice it into tiny pieces. Finely chop your parsley, too, then combine the parsley, lemon and remaining chopped garlic in a bowl, along with 2 tablespoons of olive oil.

8   Spoon this gremolata over your lamb, then serve it up.

Miso Onion Gnocchi

Serves

6

Cook time

1 hour

100g stale sourdough
or baguette

120g cashews

4 onions

3 thyme sprigs

50g pitted kalamata olives

2 tbsp tomato purée

2 garlic cloves

2 tbsp miso paste

2 tbsp dark soy sauce

900g shop-bought gnocchi

salt, pepper and olive oil

French onion soup is one of those dishes that I was shocked and appalled to discover normally contains a considerable amount of beef stock. How can a dish that seems so perfectly suited for veggies actually be very much not suitable for their consumption at all? I wanted to create a similarly punchy sauce that has all the oomph and flavour, but is totally plant-based. The glutamate found in tomatoes, miso and soy gives them a meaty flavour, making them my weapons of choice to pack a punch into the sauce. Gnocchi sometimes has the softness of foods reserved for babies, or senior citizens lacking in teeth, so the olive crumbs are important to give it a bit of crunch. You can very much make both the sauce and crumbs up to a day in advance, so throwing it together can become a miraculously speedy affair.

1   Preheat your oven to 200°C/180°C fan/gas mark 6.

2   Very finely slice your bread, then arrange the slices in a single layer on a baking sheet. Drizzle with 1 tablespoon of olive oil, then bake for 10 minutes, or until just crisp.

3   Tip your cashews into a small saucepan, and fill the pan with water to cover them. Set over a medium heat and bring to a simmer. Cook for 5 minutes to soften the cashews, then leave them to cool in the pan for 20 minutes.

4   Peel and finely slice your onions. Heat 8 tablespoons of olive oil in a sauté pan over a medium heat. Tip in your onions, then pick in your thyme leaves and add a pinch of salt. Turn the heat right down and cook the onions for about 25 minutes until they are totally soft.

5   Reduce the oven temperature to 140°C/120°C fan/gas mark 1.

6   Once your bread has crisped up, break it up with your hands and place it in a food processor. Add the olives, and pulse until you have dark breadcrumbs. Pour the breadcrumbs back onto the baking sheet and place in the oven for 30 minutes to dehydrate a bit.

7   Bring a large saucepan of water to the boil, and season it with salt as though it were a soup you were going to eat.

8   Come back to the onions. Increase the heat to medium-high, and add your tomato purée. Cook for another 10 minutes, or until the onions are really caramelised. If they look like they are catching, occasionally add a splash of water to deglaze the bottom of the pan. Peel and finely chop the garlic, then add to the pan and cook for 2 minutes longer.

9 Drain your cashews in a colander, then tip them into a blender. Add 120ml water and whizz it up to form a smooth paste. Remove 2 tablespoons of the paste and pop it aside in a bowl. Add your onion mixture to the blender, as well as your miso paste and dark soy sauce. Pour in another 100ml water, and whizz again so you have a smooth sauce. Pour this back into your sauté pan, and bring it to a gentle simmer.

10 Tip your gnocchi into the pan of boiling water and cook until they float to the top. Lift them out with a slotted spoon, and drop them directly into the sauté pan with the sauce. Add a ladleful of the gnocchi cooking water, and stir to combine.

11 Season to taste with salt and pepper, then spoon the gnocchi into bowls. Drizzle with the reserved cashew cream and top with a sprinkle of breadcrumbs, then serve.

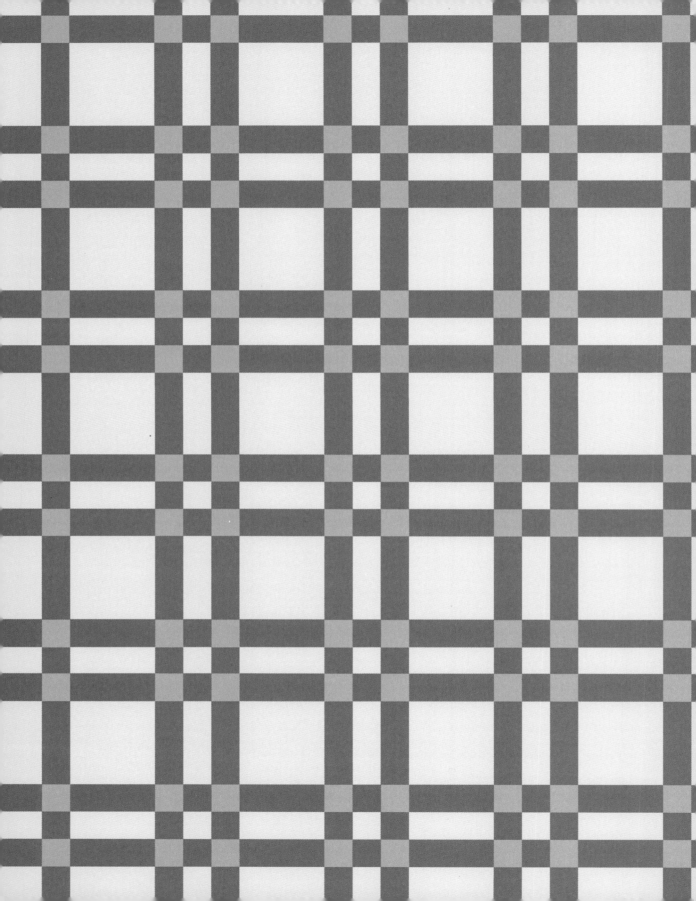

A Bit
Fancier

Calling them 'fancier' is not to say that these dishes are particularly complicated, but they have more of a show-stopping centrepiece vibe than the other recipes in this book. These are the dishes that you will be wanting to cook when you perhaps have a little more time on your hands, are after a sense of occasion and quite frankly want to show off a bit. This is where you will find the big hunks of meat and fish, as well as bits for the veggie and vegan squad. If you were cooking a big old lunch for many people, these are the dishes you would want bang in the middle of the table. To call them 'mains' would be degrading the status of the other recipes in this book, most of which are mains in their own right, but this chapter contains the roast chickens, pies, fish stews and whole sides of salmon that we so often like to champion.

Spiced Blackened Salmon Tacos with Orange Salsa

Serves
8

Cook time
45 minutes

2 tbsp sweet smoked paprika

2 tsp ground cumin

1½ tsp cayenne pepper

1 tsp dried oregano

2 tsp soft light brown sugar

2 × 600g sides of salmon

24 corn tortillas

For the salsa
1 red onion

2 red chillies

small bunch of coriander

6 oranges

salt and olive oil

There is a reason why fajita night had every family in a chokehold in the 2000s, and it is because it is a really fun way to eat. Popping lots of things in the middle of a table and getting people to help themselves is relaxed, a little chaotic, and ultimately communal – the way I like all my meals to be. These tacos look much fancier than they are, but in reality this meal involves very little cooking; all you need to do is make a zingy salsa, and grill chunky sides of salmon in spices until the flesh is charred. It would make a brilliant dinner on a weekend, but is also easy to bang together on a Wednesday night after work.

1   Spoon the paprika, cumin, cayenne pepper, dried oregano and soft brown sugar into a bowl, along with 2 teaspoons of salt and 4 tablespoons of olive oil. Mix until you have a paste.

2   Place your sides of salmon in a large baking tray, skin-sides down, and rub the spice paste all over the flesh.

3   Preheat your grill to high.

4   To make the salsa, peel and finely dice the red onion, and finely chop the red chillies. Mix together in a bowl. Roughly chop the coriander, and set it aside. Slice the top and bottom ends off the oranges so that you can stand them up flat, then work your knife around them to peel off the skin. Cut the flesh into 2cm rounds, then dice them into 1cm chunks.

5   Add the diced oranges to the bowl with the onion and chilli, along with any juices, then give it all a good mix to combine.

6   Place your salmon under the hot grill and cook for 7–8 minutes – the top will char and get a beautiful crust, while the flesh will stay tender and soft.

7   While your salmon cooks, heat your tortillas. Turn a small burner on your hob to high and place your tortillas one at a time on the grate above the flame. Cook for a few seconds on each side, turning them over with metal tongs. Keep them warm by wrapping them in a clean tea towel while you cook the rest. Alternatively, cook them for about 20 seconds on each side in a hot, dry frying pan.

8   Stir the coriander into the salsa. Pop your tortillas onto plates, and bring the salmon and salsa to the table, then let everyone serve themselves by flaking off the salmon, and adding it to their tortillas with a spoonful of salsa.

'Porchetta', But Make it Spicy

Serves
6

Cook time
3 hours, plus overnight marinating and resting

2 banana shallots

5 garlic cloves

3 lemongrass stalks

3 red chillies

1 tbsp fish sauce

1 tbsp tomato purée

1 tsp soft light brown sugar

1.4kg piece of pork belly

For the salad
1 cucumber

1 pineapple

1 red chilli

small bunch of mint

½ small bunch of coriander

1 banana shallot

3 limes

1½ tbsp fish sauce

1½ tsp soft brown sugar

salt

I use inverted commas for 'porchetta' here because this is not a traditional porchetta in many ways, but it does encapsulate the essence of one. In my mind, porchetta is a rolled-up piece of pork belly rubbed in fragrant things, and you might like to carve it up and pop it in a sandwich. This definitely ticks all of those boxes. Traditionally with porchetta, you pop a pork loin in the middle of the belly, but I find them to be so lean that they risk overcooking easily. Simply using pork belly is much more forgiving, and will give you a juicier end product. The fragrant filling borrows flavours from South East Asia – pork joins forces with her pals lemongrass, chilli and fish sauce to bring you quite the party. This would make a phenomenal alternative Sunday roast in the summertime.

1   Peel 2 shallots and your garlic, then roughly chop them. Bash your lemongrass with the base of a heavy pan, then peel off any tough outer pieces. Roughly chop the softer middles. Finely chop your chillies, seeds and all.

2   Add all these ingredients to the barrel of a small food processor, along with your fish sauce, tomato purée, sugar and 1 tablespoon of salt. Whizz it all up to a smooth paste, scraping down the edges occasionally so that it all gets blended up.

3   Place your pork belly skin-side down on a chopping board. Score the flesh in a criss-cross pattern with a sharp knife, making the cuts a few centimetres deep but ensuring you don't pierce all the way through. Rub your spice paste into the pork belly flesh, making sure you get it in all the crevices.

4   Cut 6 pieces of string to a length about double the width of the pork belly. Roll up the pork belly lengthways into a tight sausage shape, and position it with the seam-side down. Secure your pork belly roll with the pieces of string, tied into simple knots. Wrap it all tightly with cling film, then leave in the fridge overnight. This will help it to keep its shape, and also allow the seasoning to permeate throughout the meat.

5   When you're ready to cook, preheat your oven to 170°C/150°C fan/ gas mark 3½. Unwrap the pork belly, and let the skin dry out a bit while the oven warms up.

6   Place the pork seam-side down on a wire rack set over a roasting tray. Once the oven is hot, roast the pork for 2½ hours, then remove from the oven.

continues overleaf

'Porchetta', But Make it Spicy

7 Increase the oven temperature to 260°C/240°C fan/gas mark 10 or as high as your oven will go.

8 Now make your salad. Bash your cucumber with a rolling pin or heavy pan to break it up a bit, then chop it into 2cm chunks. Place in a bowl set over a sieve. Add 1 teaspoon of salt and toss it around, then set aside to let the water drain off your cucumber.

9 Cut the top off your pineapple with a serrated knife, then work your way down the sides to remove the skin. Dice the flesh into 3cm chunks.

10 Finely chop your chilli. Pick the leaves off your mint and coriander stalks, and finely chop the coriander leaves. Peel and finely slice your shallot into rounds.

11 Add your chopped chilli to a mixing bowl. Squeeze in the juice of your limes, then add the fish sauce and brown sugar. Mix it together. Add your cucumber, pineapple, shallot, mint leaves and chopped coriander, then give it a really good toss so it is all combined.

12 Place your pork back in the oven and blast it for 15 minutes, or until you have brown, crispy skin. Remove from the oven, and allow it to rest for 20 minutes.

13 Carve your pork into slices, and serve it up with your salad.

Burnt Lime and Honey Chicken Kebabs

Serves
4

Cook time
40 minutes, plus marinating

3 limes

100g honey

3 tbsp tamari

6 tbsp hot sauce (*I like Valentina, but sriracha would also be good here*)

800g skinless chicken thigh fillets

1 red onion

4 garlic cloves

2 × 400g tins of black beans

1 tsp sweet smoked paprika

½ small bunch of coriander

salt, pepper, vegetable oil and olive oil

You will need 8 wooden or metal skewers

Caramelising citrus fruits does something crazy and beautiful to their taste. The bitter notes are intensified to make a distinctly more grown-up flavour, and it makes a completely killer marinade. I whizz up burnt lime slices with their old pal honey to mellow things slightly, and it gives a seriously zingy, lip-puckering flavour that works a treat with grilled chicken. I've used tamari here to make it inclusive for gluten-free folk, but you could use light soy sauce instead if this isn't a concern for you. This would be lovely with rice or some corn tortillas, as well as the black beans you already get with it.

1 Soak 8 wooden skewers in water overnight – this will stop them burning when they cook. Alternatively, you could use metal skewers.

2 Slice 2 of your limes into thin rounds.

3 Heat 1 tablespoon of vegetable oil in a frying pan over a medium heat, then add your lime slices. Fry for about 4 minutes on each side until the flesh has caramelised.

4 Remove the lime slices from the pan and transfer to a chopping board. Roughly chop them, skins and all, then scrape it all into a blender, along with the honey, tamari, 4 tablespoons of the hot sauce, 4 tablespoons of olive oil and 1 teaspoon of salt. Whizz it up to create a smooth sauce, then spoon 2 tablespoons of it into a bowl for later.

5 Cut your chicken thigh fillets into medium-sized chunks about 4cm big. Add these to a medium-sized bowl, and pour over your marinade. Mix it so the chicken pieces are totally coated, then leave the bowl in the fridge to marinate for at least hour – overnight would be ideal, but not everyone has the luxury of this time.

6 Finely slice the red onion, and pop this into a bowl. Squeeze over the juice from the remaining lime, and sprinkle over ½ teaspoon of salt. Scrunch the onions up with your hands to encourage them to start lightly pickling, then set aside until later.

7 Once the hour is up, remove your chicken from the fridge. Thread the chicken pieces onto your soaked skewers, ensuring you don't push the pieces too close together.

8 Heat a grill or a barbecue to a medium heat. Once it is really hot, add your chicken skewers. Cook for about 12 minutes, turning them frequently so that they cook evenly.

continues overleaf

Burnt Lime and Honey Chicken Kebabs

9 While the chicken cooks, peel and finely slice your garlic cloves. Drain your black beans in a colander and give them a rinse.

10 Heat 2 tablespoons of olive oil in a medium-sized sauté pan over a medium heat. Tip in the sliced garlic, and cook it gently for a minute until it is fragrant. Add the smoked paprika and black beans, along with 250ml water, and bring to a gentle simmer. Cook for 10 minutes, smooshing down some of the black beans to create a saucy affair. Add the remaining 2 tablespoons of hot sauce, and season to taste with salt.

11 Pour any chicken cooking juices into the reserved 2 tablespoons of marinade, and give it a mix. Brush this all over your chicken skewers so they turn sticky.

12 Pop your chicken skewers on a plate, pour any remaining sauce over and scatter over your pickled red onions and coriander. Spoon your black beans into a bowl and serve alongside the chicken.

Spiced Meatballs with Dates and Chickpeas

Serves
4

Cook time
1 hour 20 minutes

For the meatballs
1 onion
80g fresh white breadcrumbs
small bunch of parsley
500g beef mince (*12 per cent fat*)
1 tsp ground cinnamon
1 tsp ground cumin
zest of 1 orange

For the sauce
1 onion
3 garlic cloves
1 large posh jar of chickpeas
(*or 2 × 400g tins*)
50g dates
3 tbsp tomato purée
1 tsp ground cumin
1 tsp ground coriander
1 tsp Aleppo chilli flakes
½ tsp ground cinnamon
300ml chicken stock
100ml thick natural yoghurt,
to serve
salt, pepper and olive oil

Meatballs have held romantic notions in my head since childhood, largely thanks to The Lady and the Tramp, *and this steaming pot of loveliness definitely has me feeling all the feels. Braising the meatballs in a spiced sauce rich with sweet dates and plump little chickpeas makes them a joy to eat and to serve to people. A hard sear on a meatball may get you a golden crust, but you lose the softness that you would otherwise get from simply poaching them in a sauce, which is why I've opted for the latter method. These ones are so tender you could eat them with a spoon.*

1   Begin by preparing the meatballs. Peel and halve the onion, then coarsely grate it and add it to a mixing bowl with your breadcrumbs. Give it a mix. The moisture from the onion will hydrate your breadcrumbs. Finely chop all but a handful of your parsley.

2   Tip your beef mince into the mixing bowl, along with the chopped parsley, followed by the cinnamon and cumin. Grate in the orange zest, then add 1 teaspoon of salt and 15 twists of black pepper. Mix with your hands so it is totally combined.

3   Weigh your mixture out into 60g portions, then roll each one into a ball using your hands and place on a tray. Leave your meatballs in the fridge to firm up while you make the sauce.

4   For the sauce, peel and finely chop your onion and garlic. Heat 8 tablespoons of olive oil in a large casserole dish over a medium heat. Add the onion and fry for 20 minutes until totally soft and just starting to caramelise.

5   Meanwhile, drain your chickpeas and give them a rinse. Finely chop your dates.

6   Add the tomato purée to the pan with the onion, and cook for 5 minutes until the whole mixture darkens. Add the garlic, cumin, coriander, Aleppo chilli flakes and cinnamon, and cook for a minute longer. Now tip in your chickpeas, dates and chicken stock, then bring the whole mixture to a simmer.

7   Nestle your meatballs into the sauce, then reduce the temperature to low. Pop on a lid and leave to simmer for 15 minutes, flipping the meatballs halfway through so they cook evenly.

8   Season your sauce to taste with salt, then sprinkle with your reserved parsley leaves. Serve topped with dollops of yoghurt.

Curried Chicken Legs with Cheesy Polenta

Serves

4

(Gf)

Cook time

1 hour

2 onions

1 tsp cumin seeds

2 tbsp curry powder

4 chicken legs

lime wedges, *to serve*

For the polenta

200ml whole milk

150g coarse polenta

100g Cheddar

30g butter

For the curry butter

3 garlic cloves

1 red chilli

140g butter

1 tsp cumin seeds

small bunch of fresh
curry leaves

1 tsp kashmiri chilli powder
(or mild chilli powder)

salt and olive oil

If you aren't really sure if you like polenta, it is probably for one of two reasons. Either you've let it firm up into a concrete-esque slab by serving it on a cold plate, or you have failed to zhuzh it up with enough dairy to make it soft and gooey. In this recipe, I will show you how to rectify both these things, by serving it on a hot platter and loading it with not one, not two, but THREE types of dairy. Many things are phenomenal eaten on top of it, but my choice for this recipe is crispy chicken legs and a generous drizzle of curried butter. If you weren't converted already, hopefully this could do it for you.

1 Preheat your oven to 220°C/200°C fan/gas mark 7.

2 Peel and halve your onions, then cut them into wedges. Arrange in a roasting tray, and sprinkle over your cumin seeds, curry powder and ½ teaspoon of salt. Drizzle with 2 tablespoons of olive oil and give it a good mix so that the onions are covered in the spices.

3 Rub 2 tablespoons of olive oil and 1 teaspoon of salt over the skin of your chicken legs, and arrange these on top of the onions. Roast in the oven for 45 minutes, or until the skins are really crispy.

4 Meanwhile, prepare the polenta. Pour your milk into a large saucepan, along with 550ml water. Bring the mixture to a simmer over a medium-high heat, then season with 1 teaspoon of salt. Once it is simmering, pour in your polenta in a steady stream, whisking continuously so the mixture doesn't clump.

5 Reduce the heat to low and leave to simmer for about 30 minutes, stirring it every couple of minutes to ensure it doesn't stick.

6 Warm up a serving platter or individual plates – this will stop the polenta from solidifying too quickly after serving.

7 When the chicken and polenta are both 5 minutes away from being ready, make your curry butter. Peel and finely slice your garlic, and finely slice your red chilli. Melt the butter in a medium-sized frying pan over a medium heat. When melted, add the garlic, cumin seeds, curry leaves and red chilli. Fry gently for about 2 minutes, until your cumin seeds and curry leaves are popping, and the butter is foaming.

8 Take the pan off the heat, and add your chilli powder.

9 Finish off your polenta. Grate the Cheddar and stir it into the polenta mixture, along with the butter, letting everything melt in.

10 Spoon the polenta onto your plates, and arrange your onions and crispy chicken on top. Spoon over the sizzling curry butter and serve with lime wedges for squeezing.

Green Harissa Spinach Pie

Serves
6

Cook time
1 hour

700g frozen whole-leaf spinach

250g ricotta

1 egg

200g feta

1 tsp dried mint

50g butter

6 filo pastry sheets

1 tbsp sesame seeds

For the green harissa

1 green pepper

3 green chillies

1 tsp cumin seeds

small bunch of parsley,
stalks and all

small bunch of coriander,
stalks and all

1 garlic clove

zest and juice of 1 lemon

salt

Tip

This is lovely eaten at room temperature, too, so can easily be cooked a day or two in advance.

There is no pastry more forgiving than filo, making this a very stress-free pie to cook up. Frozen whole-leaf spinach is a staple for me, and forms the bulk of the filling – it is so affordable when compared to fresh spinach, and there is none of that demoralising wilting and draining involved, where you are left with a sad fistful after busying yourself with several plentiful bags. I like eating this spanakopita-esque pie as part of a summery spread, or as a light lunch on a weekend.

1 Place your spinach in a large bowl, pour over warm water and leave to defrost. Preheat your oven to 210°C/190°C fan/gas mark 6½.

2 Make your green harissa. Preheat your grill to high. Place your green pepper and green chillies on a baking tray, and pop them under the grill. Cook for about 10 minutes, turning occasionally so that they char evenly. Leave them to cool slightly.

3 Toast your cumin seeds in a dry frying pan over a medium heat for 1 minute until fragrant.

4 Peel the skins off your chillies and green pepper, then remove the stalks. Scoop the seeds out of the pepper. Tip the pepper flesh and the whole chillies into a food processor. Add the parsley, coriander, garlic clove, cumin seeds, lemon zest and juice with 4 tablespoons of olive oil. Whizz into a smooth green sauce, then season with salt to taste.

5 Once your spinach has defrosted, drain it, then squeeze out all the moisture with your hands. Add this to a large bowl, then tip in your green harissa paste, followed by the ricotta. Break in the egg, then crumble in the feta and sprinkle in the dried mint. Give the whole thing a really good mix to combine.

6 Melt your butter in a small bowl in the microwave, or in a small saucepan over a low heat. Brush a 32 × 25cm baking dish with some of the melted butter. Layer four sheets of filo into the dish, arranging them widthways across the dish and brushing with the butter mixture between each layer, ensuring there is plenty of pastry hanging over the edges. Lay one sheet on top lengthways, brushing with butter again.

7 Pour your filling into the dish, then brush the final sheet of filo with butter and place on the top. Brush the surface of the filo with butter, then fold in your overhanging edges, brushing each layer with butter as you go. Using a serrated knife, cut the pie into 8 rectangular pieces. Sprinkle with sesame seeds, then bake for 30 minutes.

8 Let it cool to room temperature before serving.

Smoky Prawn Grilled Peppers with Manchego

Serves
4

Cook time
1 hour

4 Romano peppers

For the filling
2 banana shallots

2 garlic cloves

330g peeled raw king prawns

25g butter

150ml double cream,
plus 1 tbsp to serve

½ tsp hot smoked paprika

small bunch of chives

110g Manchego

For the sauce
30g butter

3 tbsp tomato purée

25g plain flour

1 tsp hot smoked paprika

1 tbsp sweet smoked paprika

400ml vegetable stock

2 tbsp double cream

salt, pepper and olive oil

By the sea in San Sebastian, I once ate a dish that I now think I may have imagined, as I have never found any trace of it since – online, in restaurants or in recipe books. It consisted of little grilled peppers, peeled and stuffed with crab, and nestled in a creamy, paprika-spiked sauce, before being grilled again. Though I've seen many recipes for pimientos rellenos, none have entirely matched what I ate that day, so I've taken the liberty of letting my imagination run away with me and developed something similar. I've stuffed the peppers with prawns instead, as I find them to be more of a crowd-pleaser than crab, not to mention a bit cheaper. The method is uncomplicated, but my word, is it a show-stopper. I'd serve this up for a summer dinner in the garden, on a table littered with flickering candles and crisp white wine. Pair with a sharp salad and lots of bread for mopping up the juices.

1   Preheat your grill to high. Add your Romano peppers to a baking dish, then rub them all over with 1 tablespoon of olive oil. Pop them under the grill for 10 minutes, turning them frequently so that they char and soften on all sides. Once they are totally soft, set them aside to cool.

2   To make the filling, peel, halve and finely slice your shallots. Peel and finely chop your garlic. Finely chop your prawns to a mince-like texture.

3   Melt the butter in a sauté pan over a medium heat. Tip in your shallots and cook them for 10 minutes until they soften. Add the garlic and cook for a minute more, then stir in your prawns, along with the cream and hot smoked paprika. Reduce the heat to low and simmer gently for 8 minutes.

4   Finely chop your chives, and add all but a handful of it to the prawn mixture. Grate in 60g of the Manchego, then season the prawns to taste with salt and 10 twists of black pepper.

5   To make your sauce, melt the butter in a medium-sized saucepan over a medium heat. Once foaming, add the tomato purée, and cook this out for 5 minutes until the mixture is dark and smells nutty. Tip in your flour, along with the hot smoked paprika and the sweet smoked paprika. Mix to form a paste and cook for 2 minutes.

continues overleaf

6 Gradually pour in your vegetable stock in small increments, beating between each addition to ensure that you have a smooth mixture before adding more stock. Once all the stock has been added, bring the mixture to a boil, and simmer it gently until the sauce thickens. Stir in 1 tablespoon of the cream, and season to taste with salt. Set aside.

7 When your peppers are cool enough to handle, carefully peel off their skins without breaking them too much, ensuring the stalks stay intact. Tear an incision down the middle of each pepper (or utilise an accidental tear!) to create a pocket, then remove and discard the seeds.

8 Pour your sauce into a baking dish, then nestle in your peppers, cut-side up. Spoon the prawn mixture into your peppers, folding the pepper flesh over at the edges to restore their pepper-like shape. Sprinkle over the remaining 50g of Manchego, focusing it mainly on the prawns. Put the tray under the grill for 5 minutes, or until it is all hot and bubbly.

9 Spoon over the remaining tablespoon of double cream, and sprinkle over the reserved chives. Serve.

Coconut and Chilli Beef Shin Pie

Serves
6

Cook time
5 hours, plus cooling

1 tsp cumin seeds

1 tsp coriander seeds

1kg beef shin

4 shallots

4 garlic cloves

3cm knob of ginger

2 lemongrass stalks

2 red chillies

½ lime

1 tbsp tomato purée

400ml coconut milk

20g soft light brown sugar

2 tbsp dark soy sauce

1 cinnamon stick

2 star anise

500g puff pastry

1 egg

½ tsp ground turmeric

salt and vegetable oil

Pie is a very romantic food to me. Early in our relationship, my partner Cam and I fell into a routine of making pies together. We'd potter to a fancy butcher's on an autumn day and braise some meat in lots of wine, dancing around the kitchen while it cooked. You have to put the time in when making a pie, but it is a gentle and calming process, and the result warms your soul in a gorgeous way. Much like a relationship, eh! This pie borrows flavours from a Malaysian rendang, but it is cooked slightly differently to make it a saucier situation.

1 Preheat your oven to 170°C/150°C fan/gas mark 3½.

2 Toast your cumin seeds and coriander seeds in a large dry frying pan over a medium heat for 2 minutes until fragrant, then set aside.

3 Cut your beef shin into 4cm chunks. Heat a little vegetable oil in a frying pan over a high heat. Working in 3 batches, brown the beef for about 3 minutes at a time, until you get a dark caramelised crust on each piece. Set aside on a plate until later.

4 Peel and finely slice your shallots. Peel and roughly chop your garlic and ginger, then roughly chop your lemongrass and chillies. Shave the rind off your lime with a knife, and roughly chop. Add it all to a small food processor, along with the toasted spices and tomato purée. Whizz it up to make a paste, scraping the edges as you go.

5 Heat 3 tablespoons of vegetable oil in a casserole dish over a medium heat. Tip in your spice paste and cook it down for about 5 minutes until fragrant and starting to stick.

6 Add the beef to the pan, followed by the coconut milk, sugar, soy sauce, cinnamon stick and star anise. Season with 1 teaspoon of salt and 10 twists of black pepper, and bring to a gentle simmer. Pop a lid on the pan, then get it in the oven. Cook for 4 hours, then let it cool for at least 30 minutes (I often cook this part the day before, and leave it to chill in the fridge overnight).

7 When you're ready to bake, increase the oven temperature to 220°C/200°C fan/gas mark 7. Roll out your puff pastry to about 2mm thick. In a small bowl, beat the egg with the turmeric.

8 Spoon the beef into a 26cm round pie dish and brush the rim with egg wash. Top with your pastry. Trim away any excess, then press down the edges with a fork to seal. Brush with your egg wash, then pop in the fridge for at least 15 minutes, or longer if you have it.

9 Remove the pie from the fridge, brush it with one more layer of egg wash, then bake for 25 minutes on the middle shelf. Serve piping hot.

Squash, Cheddar and Chilli Cake

Serves

8

Cook time

2 hours, plus cooling

1 butternut squash
(roughly 800g)

2 banana shallots

2 green chillies *(1 optional)*

80g butter, *plus extra
for greasing*

1 tsp cumin seeds

½ tsp black mustard seeds

80g plain flour

800ml whole milk

150g mature Cheddar

½ tsp kashmiri chilli powder
(or mild chilli powder)

5 eggs

salt, pepper and olive oil

The concept of a savoury cake may seem an unusual one, but trust me when I say this is gorgeous. Similar to an Italian sformato, I like to think of this as part Basque cheesecake, with a burnished top and creamy middle, and part quiche without the crust. The technique is simple: you beat eggs into a cheesy, spiced bechamel, toss through some squash, and bake it to form a silky, custardy delight. Be patient and give it time to set – this will ensure you get a phenomenal texture.

1   Preheat your oven to 220°C/200°C fan/gas mark 7.

2   Peel your squash, then cut it in half and scoop out the seeds. Chop the flesh into 2cm chunks. Tip these onto a baking tray, then drizzle with 1 tablespoon of olive oil and season with 1 teaspoon of salt. Toss it all to combine, then bake for 30 minutes, giving the squash chunks a toss halfway through so they cook evenly.

3   While your squash cooks, move on to making the base of the cake. Peel and finely slice your shallots, and finely chop 1 of the green chillies, seeds and all.

4   Melt your butter in a large saucepan over a medium heat. Once it has melted, tip in your cumin seeds, black mustard seeds, sliced shallots and green chilli. Cook for 10 minutes until the shallots have totally softened.

5   Tip your flour into the pan and cook it out for 2 minutes, then gradually pour in your milk in small increments, whisking all the while to ensure you have a totally smooth mixture before the next addition. Once all the milk has been added, bring to the boil, then reduce the heat to low and let it simmer for 3 minutes until the sauce thickens.

6   Take the pan off the heat and grate in the Cheddar. Add the chilli powder, 20 twists of black pepper and season to taste with salt, then give it a mix until it is all combined.

7   By now, the squash should have finished roasting. Remove from the oven and reduce the temperature to 180°C/160°C fan/gas mark 4.

8   Butter a 23cm springform cake tin and line it with baking parchment.

continues overleaf

Squash, Cheddar and Chilli Cake

9 Beat the eggs in a bowl, then whisk these into your cheese mixture. Tip in your roasted squash and stir.

10 Pour this mixture into your prepared cake tin, then bake for 40 minutes. After 40 minutes, increase the temperature to 200°C/180°C fan/gas mark 6 and cook it for another 10 minutes. It should be set around the edges, but still have a nice wobble in the middle.

11 While your cake cooks, finely slice your remaining green chilli, if using.

12 Allow your cake to cool for 25 minutes, then release the springform casing. Top with the green chilli, if you like, then slice and serve.

Sticky Lamb Meatball Chaat

Serves
4

Cook time
40 minutes, plus chilling

1 red onion

40g fresh breadcrumbs

½ small bunch of coriander

500g lamb mince
(20 per cent fat)

1 tsp ground cumin

½ pomegranate

juice of 1 lime

1 garlic clove

200g thick natural yoghurt

½ small bunch of mint

4 tbsp tamarind sauce
(I like the Maggi one)

40g sev *(tiny pieces of crispy chickpea noodles – if you can't find it, Bombay mix would work here)*

1 tsp chaat masala *(optional)*

flatbreads, *to serve*

salt, pepper and vegetable oil

Pictured overleaf

Tip

Chaat masala is a tangy spice mix containing mango powder and many other fun things, and it takes this somewhere really special – seek it out online, or in the 'world foods' section of a supermarket.

Chaat can come in many forms, but is generally a savoury street-food snack found on many roadsides across India, loaded up with crispy textures, tangy sauces and vibrant toppings. Most meals are improved by such things, and this absolutely goes for fat lamb meatballs too. Loading them up with all the funky, fresh flavours and making it look pretty on a platter makes a gorg meal that transports you somewhere much more exciting. Are you in your kitchen in the depths of winter in Peckham, or in a café on a balmy evening in Mumbai? Who's to say?

1 Peel your red onion, then grate half of it into a medium-sized bowl. Add your breadcrumbs and give it a mix. Leave them to sit and hydrate in the onion's moisture for 5 minutes.

2 Roughly chop all but a handful of your coriander and add to the bowl, along with the lamb mince and ground cumin. Season with 1 teaspoon of salt and 20 twists of black pepper, then combine well with your hands to get it all mixed together.

3 Roll the mixture into 12 equal-sized balls about 55g each. Pop them on a plate in the fridge to chill for a bit.

4 Now move on to the fresh elements. Deseed your pomegranate half, and add the seeds to a bowl. Finely chop your remaining red onion half, and add this to the bowl with the seeds. Squeeze in half the lime juice and give it all a mix, then set aside.

5 Peel your garlic clove, then grate it into a bowl. Add the yoghurt and the remaining lime juice, and stir to combine.

6 Pick your mint leaves. Roughly chop the remaining coriander leaves.

7 Heat 2 tablespoons of vegetable oil in a frying pan over a medium heat. Add half the meatballs and fry for about 5 minutes until they are browned on all sides. Add 150ml water, and let them steam and simmer for another 5 minutes, then remove from the pan and set aside on a plate. Repeat with the rest of the meatballs.

8 Swoosh your garlicky yoghurt onto a serving plate, then pop your meatballs on top. Drizzle over the tamarind sauce, then scatter over the mint and coriander leaves. Spoon over the red onion and pomegranate mixture, followed by the sev, and sprinkle it all with chaat masala, if using. Serve it up with some warm flatbreads to swoop through it.

Tikka Paneer

Serves

6

Cook time

45 minutes, plus marinating

1 tsp coriander seeds

1 tsp cumin seeds

4 garlic cloves

4cm knob of ginger

70g thick natural yoghurt

1 tsp kashmiri chilli powder
(or mild chilli powder)

1 tsp garam masala

½ tsp ground turmeric

1 tbsp tomato purée

2 tbsp mango chutney

450g paneer *(I like
the Apetina one)*

Bombay Slaw (opposite),
to serve

salt and vegetable oil

*You will need 10 wooden
or metal skewers*

Pictured on pages 140–141

Paneer is one of those foods that even the most staunch carnivores cannot resist. It stands up to a spice marinade ludicrously well, and it really takes to the heat of a grill like a duck to water. If possible, get the fresh stuff rather than the rubbery, squeaky stuff, as this makes for a far more pleasurable textural experience. Serve these bad boys up with the Bombay Slaw opposite, and you have a very good summer lunch on your hands.

1 Soak 10 wooden skewers in water overnight – this will stop them burning when they cook. Alternatively, you could use metal skewers.

2 Toast the coriander seeds and cumin seeds in a small, dry frying pan over a medium heat for 2 minutes until fragrant. Tip your toasted spices into a blender, and whizz them up to a fine powder.

3 Peel and roughly chop your garlic, and roughly chop your ginger. Add these to your blender too, along with the yoghurt, chilli powder, garam masala, turmeric, tomato purée and mango chutney, as well as 2 teaspoons of salt and 2 tablespoons of vegetable oil. Blend until you have a smooth mixture.

4 Chop your paneer into 2.5cm cubes. Tip these into a bowl, and pour over your marinade. Give it a really good mix so that each piece of paneer is coated. Leave to marinate for 1 hour. This is a good moment to make the slaw opposite.

5 Preheat your grill to high. Thread the paneer onto your prepared skewers, then place these on a baking sheet lined with foil and pop under the grill. Grill for about 4 minutes, then flip them over and grill for 4 minutes more on the other side. If you prefer, you could cook them on a barbecue.

6 Serve up the skewers with your slaw.

Spiced Lamb Shoulder with Bombay Slaw

Serves
8

Cook time
5 hours 30 minutes,
plus marinating

1 shoulder of lamb *(about 1.8kg)*

For the marinade
1 tbsp coriander seeds

1 tbsp cumin seeds

5 cardamom pods

1 onion

4 garlic cloves

4cm knob of ginger

150g thick natural yoghurt

1½ tsp kashmiri chilli powder
(or mild chilli powder)

1 tsp ground turmeric

1 tbsp tomato purée

For the Bombay slaw
1 white cabbage

1 red onion

juice of 2 limes

400g good-quality cherry
tomatoes

1 pomegranate

1 green chilli

small bunch of mint

100g thick natural yoghurt

50g Bombay mix

salt and vegetable oil

You can learn a lot about my mum from the way that she feeds people. This is a woman who absolutely hates lamb. The smell of it makes her feel really unwell, and that is before a piece has even passed her lips. And yet, for most special-occasion family gatherings of my childhood, my mum would cook a lamb incredibly slowly in the oven overnight, effectively poisoning herself with the fumes, to give us a really special lunch. The most selfless angel! I have inherited the need to feed people slow-cooked lamb when they come round to mine, though without the dire personal consequences. I've done this spiced version a few times over Easter, with lots of delicious sides to feast on, but I can also see it being wheeled out at the height of summer, or on a chilly winter's evening.

1 Begin by making the marinade. Toast the coriander seeds and cumin seeds in a small frying pan over a medium heat for 2 minutes until fragrant, then tip into a blender.

2 Bash your cardamom pods, and remove the little black seeds from the middle. Add these to the blender too, and whizz together to break up the seeds into a coarse powder.

3 Peel and roughly chop your onion and garlic. Roughly chop your ginger. Add all of this to your blender too, along with the yoghurt, chilli powder, turmeric, tomato purée and 2 teaspoons of salt. Blend until you have a smooth mixture.

4 Place your lamb shoulder in a roasting dish, and pour the marinade all over it. Rub it in really well, then cover the dish with kitchen foil in a tent-like structure, so that it's not touching the lamb. Pop it in the fridge to marinate for at least a few hours, ideally overnight.

5 When you're ready to cook, preheat your oven to 160°C/140°C fan/ gas mark 3. Remove the lamb from the fridge and let it come to room temperature, then slow-roast for 5 hours.

6 Towards the end of the lamb's cooking time, make your slaw. Using a mandolin or a vegetable peeler, very finely slice your cabbage. Peel and finely slice your red onion too, and mix these together in a bowl.

7 Squeeze over the lime juice and season with 1 teaspoon of salt, then gently massage the mixture for a minute or two to soften the cabbage and onion slightly.

continues overleaf

Spiced Lamb Shoulder with Bombay Slaw

8 Halve your cherry tomatoes, and remove the seeds from your pomegranate. Finely chop your green chilli. Pick the leaves off your mint.

9 Increase the oven temperature to 240°C/220°C fan/gas mark 9. Remove the foil from the lamb, and return it to the oven for 15 minutes to get some colour on it.

10 Returning to your slaw, add the yoghurt to your cabbage bowl, and mix it to combine. Add the cherry tomatoes, pomegranate seeds, chilli and mint, and give it a good toss. Spoon it into a serving bowl, and top it with your Bombay mix.

11 Pop your lamb onto a serving dish, and pull the meat off the bones. It should be so soft that you could do this with a spoon. Do it at the table to enjoy the oohs and ahhs of your guests. Serve with the slaw on the side.

Life-Saving Garlicky Chicken

Serves

4

Cook time

1 hour 30 minutes, plus resting

6 bulbs of garlic

1 lemon

small bunch of tarragon

1.6kg whole chicken

bunch of thyme

500ml good-quality chicken stock

150ml white wine

75ml double cream

salt, pepper and olive oil

Calling this recipe 'life-saving' may seem hyperbolic, but a meal like this one very much did help to revive me once upon a time. I had a near-death experience as a tiny child after losing a fight with my grandparent's pond, which resulted in me eating through a tube for a couple of weeks in a medically induced coma. My mum's friend Sophie would bring food to the hospital for my parents, and the first food I ate when I woke (besides cheesy Wotsits) was her garlic roast chicken. This is my version of that meal. It is the kind of deeply nourishing dish that invigorates your whole body as you eat it, with the warmth of garlic and zing of lemon bringing life back to cold toes and weary minds. It is all cooked in one large casserole dish to create a very easy roast dinner that even the sleepiest of people could manage.

1 Preheat the oven to 170°C/150°C fan/gas mark 3½.

2 Peel all your garlic cloves (this may take a while!). Cut your lemon in half. Pick the leaves off your tarragon, keeping the stalks.

3 Get your chicken out of the fridge to bring it to room temperature.

4 Place all the garlic cloves in a large, deep casserole dish, and pick in your thyme leaves – it's okay if some small bits of stalk end up in there, but you don't want any really tough ones. Add the stock, white wine, 2 tablespoons of olive oil, 1 teaspoon of salt and 10 twists of black pepper. Place the casserole dish over a low heat and bring the mixture to a gentle simmer.

5 Stuff the cavity of your chicken with half the lemon, along with your tough thyme stalks and tarragon stalks. Rub the top of the chicken with 1 teaspoon of salt and 1 tablespoon of olive oil, then place the bird in the casserole dish on top of your garlic. Pop a piece of baking parchment on top, then cover with a lid. Put it in the oven on a low shelf to roast for 50 minutes.

6 Increase the oven temperature to 220°C/200°C fan/gas mark 7. Remove the lid and baking parchment from your dish, then roast for another 15 minutes to crisp up the skin.

7 Meanwhile, finely chop your tarragon leaves.

8 Carefully lift the chicken out of the casserole dish and set aside to rest for 20 minutes. Place the dish over a medium heat, and reduce the juices until thick enough to coat the back of a spoon. Squeeze in the juice of your remaining lemon half, then stir through your tarragon leaves and cream. Season to taste with salt and pepper.

9 Carve up your chicken, then serve it on top of your sauce.

Tip

Peeling the many, many garlic cloves is the only real effort involved here, but I would not judge you if you chose to buy pre-peeled in this instance.

Lemony Leek and Parmesan Tart

Serves
4

Cook time
45 minutes, plus resting

220g Parmesan or vegetarian
hard cheese

60g butter

½ tsp baking powder

100g plain flour, *plus extra
for dusting*

3 leeks

3 thyme sprigs

150ml vegetable stock

250g ricotta

1 small garlic clove

zest and juice of ½ lemon

salt, pepper and olive oil

Like most people my age, I was bred on Nigella Lawson recipes. There is a particular nibble of hers that we always made at Christmas: cheese stars. I had a lightning-bolt moment recently where I decided to make a tart using a similar pastry, and this is it. It's a bit of a cheese fest, with the cheesy pastry topped with lemony ricotta, and braised leeks have come along for the ride, too. It makes a dreamy light lunch in the spring.

1. Cut your Parmesan into chunks and whizz in a food processor. Remove a small amount, about 10g, and set aside. Chop your butter into pieces, and add these to the food processor too, with the baking powder, flour and 20 twists of black pepper. Pulse until it comes together like yellow breadcrumbs, adding 1 tablespoon of water if it is too crumbly – this will depend on the heat on the kitchen.

2. Tip the mixture onto a clean work surface, then knead for a minute until it comes together in a smooth dough. Wrap the dough in cling film, then pop it in the fridge to rest for 20 minutes.

3. Preheat your oven to 180°C/160°C fan/gas mark 4 and line a baking sheet with baking parchment.

4. Trim the ends off your leeks, then cut them in half widthways. Halve each leek section lengthways.

5. Lightly flour your work surface. Remove your pastry from the fridge, and roll it out into a rectangle roughly 4cm longer than your leeks, and 3mm thick. The pastry may crack – if it does, just press it back together. Trim the edges to neaten, then use a knife to lightly trace a border 2cm from the edges. Transfer to the prepared baking sheet and bake for 15 minutes, then remove it from the oven and leave it to cool – it will firm up as it does.

6. Heat 2 tablespoons of olive oil in a cast-iron skillet or sturdy frying pan over a medium-high heat. Once the pan is hot, add your leeks, cut-sides down, and cook for 3 minutes until they have a nice char. Flip them over, and cook for another 3 minutes on the other side.

7. Pick your thyme leaves into the pan and add the veg stock. Let it come to a simmer, reduce the heat to low and cover. Simmer for 10 minutes.

8. Tip your ricotta into a bowl, and grate in your garlic and lemon zest. Add the lemon juice and 2 tablespoons of olive oil. Whisk for a few minutes so the ingredients combine and it becomes smooth.

9. Once the pastry has cooled, spoon your ricotta on the centre, then spread it to the border. Arrange your leeks on top, then sprinkle over some thyme leaves and the reserved Parmesan. Serve immediately.

Crispy Duck with Port-Braised Lentils

Serves
4

Cook time
1 hour 30 minutes

4 duck legs
1 large onion
1 large carrot
2 celery sticks
1 tsp coriander seeds
1 tsp cumin seeds
2 garlic cloves
2 rosemary sprigs
3 tbsp tomato purée
300ml ruby port
800ml chicken stock
250g Puy lentils
½ bunch of parsley
salt, pepper and olive oil

For some people, lentils conjure up joyful images of steaming, spiced pots of dal. To some older folk, they may be synonymous with flavourless, plant-based stews eaten by plant-based pioneers in the 70s. To others, they are vessels for rich, meaty flavours, braised for a little while to create something unctuous. This dish is very much the latter example, inspired by cooking found in the South of France. Confit duck would be a dream here, but honestly I can rarely be bothered with the lengthy ritual of this process. Crispy roasted legs nestled into the sticky, port-rich lentils do the job just fine, and with far less effort. I'd serve this up on a cosy evening in the depths of winter, when I'm already firmly aboard the hearty food train, and follow it up with lots of games and silliness.

1 Preheat your oven to 190°C/170°C fan/gas mark 5½.

2 Heat 1 tablespoon of olive oil in a wide casserole dish over a low-medium heat. Add the duck legs, skin-side down, letting the fat render out gently for 15 minutes until your pan is glistening with duck fat and the skin is golden. Flip them over and brown for 5 minutes on the other side.

3 Peel and finely dice your onion. Finely dice your carrot and celery. Using a pestle and mortar, bash your coriander seeds and cumin seeds to break them down a bit. Peel and finely chop your garlic.

4 Transfer your duck legs from the casserole dish to a baking tray and roast in the oven for 15 minutes.

5 Add the onion, celery and carrot to the dish you used to brown the duck, along with your crushed spices and rosemary sprigs. Cook over a gentle heat for 15 minutes until the veg is all totally soft.

6 Add the tomato purée and garlic, and cook for 3 minutes until the mixture darkens.

7 Increase the heat to medium, then pour in your port. Cook for 3 minutes to let it reduce by about half, then add your chicken stock. Bring to a simmer, then tip in your lentils. Season with 1 teaspoon of salt and 5 twists of black pepper. Nestle in the duck legs, then cover with a lid and get it in the oven for 30 minutes.

8 After 30 minutes, remove the lid and increase the heat to 220°C/200°C fan/gas mark 7. Bake for another 15 minutes to crisp up that duck skin again.

9 Give your lentils a taste to check their seasoning, adding more salt and pepper if you like. Roughly chop your parsley, then scatter this over the duck and lentils. Serve.

Celeriac Schnitzel with Charred Pepper Salsa

Serves
4

Cook time
1 hour 40 minutes

1 large celeriac

2 red peppers

100g plain flour

150g panko breadcrumbs

2 preserved lemons

½ small bunch of parsley

1 tbsp sherry vinegar

½ tsp hot smoked paprika

1 garlic clove

1 large posh jar of butter beans
(or 2 × 400g tins)

juice of ½ lemon

salt, pepper, olive oil
and vegetable oil

Roasting celeriac whole gives the tenderest texture, and you can take it in all kinds of directions from there. One of my favourite ways to eat it is to dredge the slices in batter and breadcrumbs and fry them, because most things can be improved upon with a spell sizzling in some hot, hot fat. The soft, milky flesh of celeriac ends up looking remarkably like a chicken Milanese. You could prep the steaks and salsa in advance for a rapid midweek dinner, or enjoy them as part of a more substantial feast.

1   Preheat the oven to 200°C/180°C fan/gas mark 6.

2   Trim any knobbly bits off your celeriac and drizzle over 1 tablespoon of olive oil. Season with 1 teaspoon of salt, then rub it all in with your hands. Wrap the celeriac tightly in kitchen foil, then place it on a baking tray and roast for 1 hour. Leave to cool.

3   Preheat your grill to high. Place your peppers on a baking tray and grill for 10 minutes, turning frequently so they cook evenly. You want the skin to get wrinkled and slightly blackened. Pop them into a bowl, and cover it with a tea towel so the steam softens them.

4   Slice your celeriac into six 2cm thick discs. Whisk your flour in a bowl with 160ml water and 1 teaspoon salt. Pour your panko breadcrumbs into another bowl. Dip the first celeriac slice into your flour batter so that it is totally submerged, then shake off any excess and dip it into your breadcrumbs to fully coat. Set this aside on a tray and repeat with the remaining slices.

5   Once your peppers are cool enough to handle, peel off their skins. Discard their seeds and stalks, then roughly chop the flesh, and add this to a bowl. Finely chop your preserved lemons and parsley and add these to the bowl. Add the sherry vinegar and paprika, give it a mix and season to taste with salt and 10 cracks of black pepper.

6   Bash your garlic clove to remove the skin. Drain your butter beans, reserving 2 tablespoons of liquid, then rinse in a colander. Tip into a food processor, along with the garlic, lemon juice and 2 tablespoons of olive oil. Whizz to a paste and season to taste with salt, then heat it up in a saucepan.

7   Heat 8 tablespoons of vegetable oil in a large frying pan over a medium heat. Add your celeriac slices, and pan-fry for 3 minutes on each side until the breadcrumbs are crisp and golden.

8   Slice your celeriac schnitzels. Swoosh your butter bean purée around a serving plate, then top it with your sliced schnitzels. Spoon over your charred pepper salsa, then serve.

Ale-Braised Oyster Mushrooms

Serves
4

Cook time
1 hour

25g dried porcini mushrooms

1 onion

1 carrot

2 celery sticks

2 garlic cloves

3 thyme sprigs

400g oyster mushrooms
(mixture of king and regular)

15g cornflour

1 tbsp tomato purée

200ml golden ale

200g tinned chopped tomatoes

1 tbsp yeast extract
(I use Marmite)

1 tbsp dark soy sauce

1 bay leaf

1 tbsp Henderson's Relish

For the herby mash
1kg Maris Piper potatoes

90ml oat milk *(or whole milk if not making vegan)*

50g dairy-free butter *(or butter if not making vegan)*

½ small bunch of chives

salt, pepper and olive oil

Think steak-and-ale pie filling, but plant-based. The meatiness of the oyster mushrooms could fool the most ardent carnivores. I first made this dish as pie filling, and it works very well this way (topped with puff pastry) but my ultimate way to eat this is with a steaming pile of greens and my beloved mashed potato. Henderson's Relish is a brilliant condiment with all the savoury punch of Worcestershire sauce, but without the anchovies. You can find it in large supermarkets or online.

1 Tip your porcini mushrooms into a heatproof jug and pour over 300ml boiling water. Leave to soak for 30 minutes, then remove your mushrooms from the liquid (keep the liquid) and finely chop.

2 Peel and finely dice your onion. Finely dice your carrot and celery, too. Peel the garlic, and finely chop the garlic and thyme. In a bowl, toss the oyster mushrooms with cornflour and 1 teaspoon of salt.

3 Heat 1 tablespoon of olive oil in a large frying pan over a high heat. Once hot, add a few of your king oyster mushrooms and sear them hard for a few minutes until browned and softened, turning occasionally so that they cook evenly. Remove and set aside on a plate, then repeat with the rest of the oyster mushrooms.

4 Heat 4 tablespoons of olive oil in a cast-iron pot over a low-medium heat. Add the onion, carrot and celery and fry for 10 minutes until softened. Stir in the tomato purée, garlic and thyme, and cook for another 2 minutes.

5 Add the ale and cook for about 3 minutes, or until it has reduced by half. Add the chopped tomatoes, mushroom stock, chopped porcini, oyster mushrooms, yeast extract, soy sauce and bay leaf. Give it a mix and bring to a boil, then reduce the heat and simmer for 30 minutes.

6 Meanwhile, make your mash. Peel your potatoes, then chop into 5cm chunks. Pop them into a large saucepan, and fill it up with cold water. Season with 1 tablespoon of salt, then bring it to the boil. Once boiling, reduce the heat to low and simmer for 15 minutes.

7 Drain in a colander, and leave the potatoes to steam dry in there for a bit. Tip them back into the pan, and add your milk and butter. Mash with a potato masher until you have a totally smooth mixture. Chop the chives and add, then season to taste with salt and pepper.

8 Return to your mushrooms. Pick out the woody bits of thyme, then season the mixture to taste with salt and pepper. Stir through your Henderson's Relish and serve with the creamy mash.

All the Fishies Stew with Piri-Piri-oli

Serves
6

Cook time
1 hour 40 minutes

1kg mussels

200ml white wine

2 onions

2 fennel bulbs

8 medium-sized tomatoes

2 garlic cloves

2 tbsp tomato purée

1.2 litres good-quality fish stock

300g basmati rice

500g monkfish fillets

400g shell-on raw king prawns

½ small bunch parsley

juice of ½ lemon, *plus wedges
to serve*

For the piri-piri-oli
1 Romano pepper

1 red chilli

1 garlic clove

½ tsp hot smoked paprika

½ tsp dried oregano

1 tbsp apple cider vinegar

2 egg yolks

250ml vegetable oil

juice of 1 lemon

1 tsp Dijon mustard

salt, pepper and olive oil

*Not much makes me feel more boujie than eating a big bowl of fish stew:
it is coming of age on a holiday, and ordering off a three-course menu
for the first time; it is eating at restaurants well beyond your means on
seafronts in far-away places, and savouring every second of it. If you
want your pals to leave your house feeling like the classiest dudes in town,
this is the meal you want to cook them. This one is inspired by Portuguese
arroz de marisco, which also cooks pointy grains of rice into the fishy
base for starch and substance. Buy shell-on prawns so you can revel in
the unbridled joy of sucking the juice out of the heads.*

1   Start by making your piri-piri-oli. Preheat your grill to high. Place
your Romano pepper and red chilli on a baking tray, and drizzle
them with 1 tablespoon of olive oil. Pop under the grill for about
10 minutes until the skin is blackened, turning them over halfway
through. Allow to cool slightly.

2   Once cool enough to touch, peel your pepper and chilli, then add
both to a small food processor. Peel the garlic and add this too,
along with your hot smoked paprika, dried oregano and apple cider
vinegar. Whizz to form a paste, then spoon this into a bowl. Give
your food processor a rinse and dry.

3   Add your egg yolks to the food processor. Run the machine, and
gradually drizzle in your vegetable oil. When the mixture starts to
look very thick, squeeze in your lemon juice, then return to adding
your oil. If you need to loosen it more, do so with splashes of water.

4   Add your spicy pepper paste and Dijon mustard, then give it a
whizz once more. Season the mayo to taste with lots of salt, and
a touch more lemon juice if it needs more acidity – your lemons
may be smaller than mine! Set aside.

5   Pop a large saucepan with a lid over a medium heat. Look through
your mussels, discarding any with broken shells. Remove the
beards, along with any large barnacles. Add your mussels to the
pan, along with your white wine, then bring it up to a boil. Pop on
a lid, reduce the heat to low, and leave to simmer for 5 minutes.
Remove the lid and discard any mussels whose shells have not
opened. Strain the rest, reserving the liquid, and pop the mussels
into the fridge.

continues overleaf

All the Fishies Stew with Piri-Piri-oli

6 Peel and finely chop the onions. Finely chop the fennel too.

7 Heat 6 tablespoons of olive oil in a very large casserole dish or saucepan over a medium heat (you could do this in two smaller pots if you don't have a massive one). Add your onion and fennel and cook gently for 20 minutes, until both are totally soft.

8 Meanwhile, coarsely grate your tomatoes into a bowl. Peel and finely chop your garlic cloves.

9 Add your garlic to the pan, and cook for 1 minute, then tip in your grated tomatoes, along with all their juices. Stir in the tomato purée, then let it all cook down for 10 minutes until the mixture has thickened.

10 Pour your fish stock and mussel cooking liquid into the pan, and bring the mixture to a gentle simmer.

11 Tip your rice into a sieve and give it a really good rinse with cold water, then add to the pan. Reduce the heat to low and simmer it for 10 minutes.

12 Cut your monkfish into large chunks about 5cm big. Add these to the pan, along with the prawns, and simmer for 5 minutes longer. Return your mussels to the pan, and simmer for another minute.

13 Roughly chop half the parsley and add it to the broth, along with the lemon juice. Adjust the seasoning to taste.

14 Spoon the stew into bowls and top it with your piri-piri-oli and the remaining parsley leaves. Serve with lemon wedges for squeezing.

Tip

This makes more piri-piri-oli than you'll need. It will keep covered with cling film directly on its surface for 2 days and you can eat it with pretty much anything you like.

Carb City

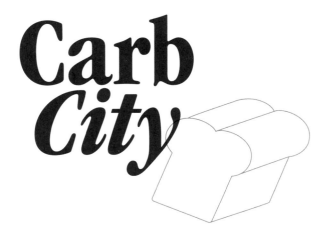

I am one of those people who doesn't think a meal is complete without carbs. There is not a culinary situation I can imagine that wouldn't benefit from a side of steaming mashed potatoes, or chewy flatbreads, or fluffy rice. This chapter is a dedication to all these foods that I frankly couldn't live without, or at least wouldn't want to. The majority of these are side dishes, though some of them are main meals – or sides tasty enough that you may want to eat them as the entirety of your dinner (see Sesame Roast Potatoes, page 167).

Spicy Lemongrass Sausage Smashburgers

Serves
4

Cook time
45 minutes

2 garlic cloves

4 spring onions

1 lemongrass stalk

1 red chilli

6 good-quality pork sausages

1 tbsp fish sauce

1 tbsp soy sauce

3 tbsp sriracha

6 tbsp mayonnaise

¼ iceberg lettuce

4 burger buns

8 squares of burger cheese

For the carrot pickle

2 large carrots

150ml rice vinegar or
white wine vinegar

2 tbsp caster sugar

½ small bunch of coriander

½ small bunch of mint

salt, pepper and vegetable oil

I find pork to be one of the winning meats when it comes to standing up to big personalities like chilli, lemongrass and fish sauce, which makes sausage meat an ideal candidate to form the patties of these incredibly punchy burgers. The fattiness of the meat and the sweet, plasticky cheese are offset with heat, along with a hit of sharpness from the carrot pickle. This is well and truly my favourite burger I have ever developed.

1   Begin with the carrot pickle. Peel your carrots, then julienne them. Pour your vinegar into a medium-sized heatproof bowl, along with the sugar, 150ml water and ½ teaspoon of salt. Pop this in the microwave and cook for 1 minute until steaming. Alternatively, heat in a small saucepan. Now add your carrots to the liquid, then leave them to sit and pickle for at least 30 minutes; ideally longer, if you have time. Pick the leaves off your coriander and mint.

2   Meanwhile, make your patties. Peel your garlic, and finely chop your garlic, spring onions, lemongrass and red chilli – you could do this in a small food processor if you have one.

3   Squeeze your sausage meat into a bowl, then add your chopped aromatics. Pour in the fish sauce and soy sauce and season with ½ teaspoon of salt, then give it all a really good mix with your hands. Divide your mixture into 8 equal-sized portions.

4   Combine your sriracha and mayonnaise in a bowl, and finely slice your iceberg lettuce.

5   Heat a large frying pan over a high heat. Halve your burger buns, then toast them, cut-side down, in the dry pan for a few minutes, or until golden. Remove your buns from the pan and set them aside.

6   Add 2 tablespoons of vegetable oil to the same pan. Once it's really hot, add half your sausage patties to the pan, ensuring they are spaced well apart. Place a square of baking parchment on top. Using the base of a heavy-bottomed pan, press down hard on each sausage-mixture portion to flatten them. Remove the parchment and continue to fry the patties for 2 minutes before flipping them over. Add a piece of burger cheese to the top of each, then place a lid on the pan and fry for 2 minutes more. Set aside and keep warm while you repeat with the rest of the burgers.

7   Returning to the carrot pickle, drain your carrots, then stir in the coriander and mint leaves.

8   Spoon 1 tablespoon of your sriracha mayo on the tops and bottoms of each bun. Add a handful of lettuce to the bases, stack two patties on each, then top with herby carrot pickle. Add the lids and serve.

Halloumi Rostis with Tzatziki

Makes
12 rostis

Cook time
1 hour

500g Maris Piper potatoes

1 cucumber

225g halloumi

½ small bunch of dill

1 small garlic clove

300g thick Greek yoghurt

1 tsp dried mint

juice of ½ lemon, *plus wedges to serve*

salt, pepper and rapeseed oil

A hash brown is something of a sacred thing in the Wyburd household. From freezer-aisle ones cooked up by my dad for full English breakfasts, to McDonald's ones picked up from the Drive-Thru on the motorway, they are happy and frequent food punctuations in my life. A rosti is basically a posh hash brown in my books, and I was pleased to discover that grating halloumi into the mixture not only seasons them to perfection, but also aids them in getting very golden and crispy. Make them for brunch, for lunch, for any time of day you'd like to be joyful, basically.

1 Peel your potatoes, and grate them on the coarsest side of your box grater. Add the grated potatoes to a large bowl, cover with water, and leave to soak for 20 minutes.

2 Meanwhile, grate your cucumber on the coarsest side. Add this to a sieve set over a bowl, and sprinkle with 1 teaspoon of salt. Leave to sit above the bowl for 20 minutes so that excess liquid can drain.

3 Get that grater out again, and grate your block of halloumi.

4 Finely chop your dill, then peel and grate your garlic.

5 Drain your grated potatoes, then tip into a clean tea towel. Twist the top so that the potato forms a ball in the middle, then squeeze out all that excess liquid over the sink.

6 Tip your grated potatoes back into a clean bowl, then add the halloumi. Season with ¾ teaspoon of salt, then give it all a good mix. This is your rosti mixture.

7 Heat 4 tablespoons of rapeseed oil in a large frying pan over a medium-high heat. Working in batches, add your rosti mixture in golf ball-sized handfuls, flattening them down with a spatula. Top with a piece of baking parchment, then place a heavy-bottomed pan on top to press them down. Fry for about 5–7 minutes, or until the base of each rosti is deeply crispy and golden.

8 Remove the pan and parchment, then flip your rostis over and cook for 5–7 minutes on the other side, this time without the pan on top. When they are cooked, remove your rostis from the pan and keep warm in a low oven while you cook the rest.

9 Come back to your cucumber. Squeeze to remove any excess liquid, then tip the cucumber into a bowl. Add the yoghurt, chopped dill, garlic, dried mint and lemon juice and give it a good mix, then season with ½ teaspoon of salt.

10 Dollop your tzatziki onto a plate, then stack your rostis next to it. Serve with lemon wedges for squeezing.

Charred Corn and Coconut Pilaf

Serves
4 as a main, 6 as a side

Cook time
50 minutes

1 onion

3 garlic cloves

2cm knob of ginger

1 tsp cumin seeds

½ tsp black mustard seeds

350g basmati rice

½ tsp ground turmeric

½ tsp kashmiri chilli powder
(or mild chilli powder)

400ml coconut milk

4 corns on the cob

½ small bunch of coriander

1 red chilli

50g coconut flakes

salt, coconut oil and
vegetable oil

Rice is one of the most versatile accompaniments out there. It goes with virtually any meal. It is a lovely, fluffy canvas for any flavour. While this coconutty charred corn number would be lovely with a curry, it would also be phenomenal with a roast chicken, braised lamb, or any number of summery salads. It also makes a fantastic meal on its own. If you aren't cooking during high summer, use frozen corn on the cob instead of fresh.

1   Peel, halve and finely chop your onion. Peel and finely chop your garlic and ginger, too.

2   Heat 3 tablespoons of coconut oil in a large sauté pan with a lid over a medium heat. Tip in your cumin seeds and mustard seeds and cook for 1 minute – they will pop and sizzle – then tip in your chopped onion. Cook for about 20 minutes, or until it is totally soft.

3   Meanwhile, tip the rice into a sieve. Rinse until the water runs clear.

4   Add your garlic, ginger, turmeric and chilli powder to the pan with the onion, and cook for 2 minutes more, then tip in the rice. Add the coconut milk, along with 200ml water and 1 teaspoon of salt, then bring the mixture to a simmer. Reduce the heat to as low as possible, then pop on a lid and let it gently cook for 15 minutes.

5   Meanwhile, heat a cast-iron skillet or griddle pan over a high heat. Rub your corn all over with 1 tablespoon of vegetable oil, then add to the pan. Cook the corn cobs for about 8 minutes, turning them frequently so they char evenly. Remove from the pan and set aside.

6   Once the rice's cooking time is up, turn off the heat and leave to sit for 10 minutes, leaving the lid on so the rice can finish cooking in the steam. This step is essential for fluffy rice.

7   Stand your corn cobs on their ends, and carefully carve off the kernels with a sharp knife. Roughly chop your coriander leaves and finely slice the red chilli.

8   Heat 2 tablespoons of coconut oil in a frying pan over a medium heat, then add your sliced chilli and coconut flakes. Fry for a minute or so, until the coconut flakes just turn golden.

9   Remove the lid from your rice, and gently fluff the grains with a fork. Fold through your charred corn, then spoon over your chilli and coconut flakes and scatter over the coriander. Serve.

Sesame Roast Potatoes

Serves
8

Cook time
1 hour 20 minutes

2.5kg Maris Piper potatoes
2 tbsp sesame seeds
1 tsp sweet smoked paprika
½ tsp caster sugar
salt and olive oil

It would be bold to claim that a simple, perfectly cooked roast potato could be improved upon, but something about this sprinkle is so magical that it might just propel me to make such a statement. I learned from the brilliant Saskia Sidey that combining toasted sesame seeds, smoked paprika, salt and sugar creates a flavour incredibly reminiscent of pork crackling. Sprinkling this over crispy roast potatoes when they are done doing their thing in the oven creates the most moreish little bites that make a phenomenal side to any meal.

1 Peel your potatoes. Chop large ones into quarters, medium-sized ones in half, and leave small ones as they are. Add them to a large saucepan, then fill the pan with cold water so that all the potatoes are covered. Season the water to taste with salt as though it were a soup – this is important to make your potatoes taste good!

2 Pop your pan over a medium heat, and bring it up to a boil. Once boiling, simmer your potatoes for 15 minutes, or until tender.

3 Preheat your oven to 220°C/200°C fan/gas mark 7.

4 When your potatoes are cooked, tip them into a colander and leave them to steam dry in the sink for a couple of minutes. Shake them briefly in the colander to break down the edges a little.

5 While your potatoes steam dry, pour 10 tablespoons of olive oil into a large roasting tray. Put this in the oven to heat up for 3 minutes.

6 Remove the tray from the oven, then tip in your potatoes. Return to the oven and roast for 1 hour, tossing the potatoes every 20 minutes or so to ensure they crisp up evenly. If some are done before others, remove them from the tray and pop on a plate, returning them to the oven 5 minutes before the rest are done to warm through. Resist the urge to eat them.

7 While your potatoes cook, make your smoky sesame powder. Pour your sesame seeds into a dry frying pan, and toast them for 5 minutes until they are a deep golden brown.

8 Using a pestle and mortar, bash the toasted sesame seeds to form a crumb. Add your smoked paprika, sugar and 1 teaspoon of salt, then mix to combine.

9 Once your potatoes are cooked, sprinkle the dust all over and serve.

Curried Potato Salad

Serves
6 as a side

Cook time
45 minutes, plus cooling

300ml rapeseed oil, *for frying*

**small bunch of fresh
curry leaves**

1 tsp cumin seeds

½ tsp black mustard seeds

1 tsp garam masala

½ tsp ground turmeric

½ tsp kashmiri chilli powder
(or mild chilli powder)

1.2kg Charlotte potatoes

400g tin of chickpeas

1 red onion

juice of 1 lemon

1 garlic clove

1 tsp apple cider vinegar

1 tsp mustard powder

small bunch of coriander

salt

Potato salad is an essential part of any British summertime spread. It is a dish I always shotgun making for a potluck, and I have spent many years perfecting the classic version (lots of cornichons, dill and lemon). I reckon most people have their own way of doing it that they know and love, so this is an alternative I have started making in recent years. The beauty is that the mayonnaise comes together with a stick blender as if by magic, and uses the water from a tin of chickpeas to keep it a plant-based. Fear not: it has all the creaminess of a regular mayo, but uses a by-product you often chuck down the sink. For once, the chickpeas themselves are left aside, but you can find plenty of other uses for them in this book.

1   Pour your rapeseed oil into a saucepan over a low heat. Bring it to 180°C, then turn off the heat. If you don't have a thermometer, you can test it out by dropping in a cumin seed. If it sizzles, it is hot enough. Add your curry leaves, cumin seeds, mustard seeds, garam masala, turmeric and chilli powder to the oil, then leave at room temperature. The aromatics will infuse the oil as it cools.

2   Meanwhile, halve the potatoes and add them to a large saucepan. Pour over boiling water, then season the water to taste with salt as though it were a soup. Bring to the boil, then simmer for 15 minutes, or until the potatoes are tender. Drain, then allow them to cool to room temperature.

3   Open the tin of chickpeas and strain the liquid into a bowl. Set this aside for later. Save the chickpeas for another time.

4   Peel and finely slice your red onion. Add it to another bowl with half the lemon juice and a pinch of salt. Scrunch it up in your hands to lightly pickle it.

5   Once your oil has cooled to room temperature, strain to remove the aromatics, then set aside the crispy bits for later.

6   Measure 120ml of your chickpea liquid into a jug. Grate in your garlic, then add the apple cider vinegar, along with the cooled infused oil, mustard powder, remaining lemon juice and 1 teaspoon of salt. Whizz with a stick blender to emulsify the mixture. It should turn thick and creamy. Adjust the seasoning if needed.

7   Tip your potatoes into a big mixing bowl, then pour in your mayonnaise. Add all but a handful of your pickled red onion, and give it all a really good mix.

8   Spoon your potato salad into a serving bowl. Pick the leaves off the coriander and add on top of the salad, along with your remaining pickled onions and the crispy curry leaf bits from your oil. Serve.

All the Pickles Potato Salad

Serves
6 as a side

Cook time
50 minutes

750g baby potatoes

small bunch of mint

2 small bunches of parsley

60g capers, *plus 3 tbsp brine from the jar*

50g cornichons

4 pickled guindilla chillies

juice of 1 lemon

1 tbsp Dijon mustard

4 spring onions

200g fine green beans

salt, pepper and olive oil

A creamy potato salad is nice and all, but I love one dressed in a zingy, herby sauce just as much. It cuts through the fatty things you'd often find on a barbecue in the most glorious of ways. Like the millennial cliché I am, I eat a lot of pickled things, and jars of them dominate my fridge shelves. They do come in very handy when it comes to bringing some acidity to the party – here found in the form of capers, cornichons and pickled chillies. Mix and match the quantities of each depending on what you have in the fridge, and how spicy you like things.

1   Bring a large pan of water to a boil, and salt it as though it were a soup. While it comes up to a simmer, cut your potatoes in half. Once the water is simmering, add your potatoes, and cook them for 12 minutes.

2   Meanwhile, make your dressing. Pick the leaves off your mint, then roughly chop them, along with your parsley (stalks and all), capers, cornichons and pickled chillies. Add all of this to a food processor, along with your lemon juice, Dijon mustard and 12 tablespoons of olive oil. Add the caper brine, then whizz it all up until you have a chunky green dressing.

3   Finely slice your spring onions, then fold these through the mixture. Season to taste with salt and pepper.

4   When the potatoes have been cooking for 12 minutes, add your green beans to the pan and cook them together for 3 minutes. Check that the potatoes are tender with a fork, then drain both in a colander. Let them steam dry and cool for 15 minutes.

5   Pour your potatoes and beans into your chosen serving bowl, then add the dressing. Give it all a really good toss to combine. Serve.

Cheesy Spring Onion and Potato Pie

Serves
6

Cook time
2 hours

85g cold butter

200g mature Cheddar

165g plain flour, *plus extra for dusting*

3 thyme sprigs

1 tbsp whole milk

1.2kg Maris Piper potatoes

1 onion

6 spring onions

300ml double cream

salt, pepper and olive oil

This one is a proper double-carb party. I've fully embraced British flavours here, with spring onion and Cheddar putting in a really good shift to flavour the potato-y middle of the pie. This would be phenomenal as a weekend lunch served with a sharp salad, or as the carby accompaniment to a roast chicken. The cheese in the pastry will make it darken more than regular shortcrust, so don't be alarmed.

1 Start by dicing your butter into very small cubes, then pop it back into the fridge to stay cold. Grate your Cheddar, and syphon off 30g for the pastry.

2 Add this 30g of Cheddar to a food processor, along with the butter and flour. Pick in the thyme leaves and season with ½ teaspoon of salt. Pulse until the mixture resembles yellow breadcrumbs. Add your milk and pulse again until it starts to clump together.

3 Tip your pastry out onto a clean work surface, then briefly work it so it comes together into a smooth dough. Wrap it in cling film, and pop it in the fridge to chill for 15 minutes.

4 Preheat your oven to 200°C/180°C fan/gas mark 6.

5 Meanwhile, peel your potatoes, and finely slice them on a mandolin. Peel and finely slice your onion, then finely slice your spring onions into rounds, too.

6 Remove your pastry from the fridge, and lightly dust a clean work surface with flour. Roll out the pastry to a thickness of about 2mm.

7 Line a 20cm springform cake tin with your pastry, pushing it right into the sides of the tin into an even layer that goes most of the way up the sides. Line it with baking parchment, then fill with baking beans (or dried beans/rice). Blind-bake the pastry for 12 minutes, then carefully remove the baking beans and parchment, and bake the pastry case for 5 minutes more.

8 To make your filling, heat 4 tablespoons of olive oil in a large frying pan over a medium heat. Add the onion and potatoes and fry for about 15 minutes, moving them around a little so that they cook evenly.

continues overleaf

Cheesy Spring Onion and Potato Pie

9   Pour in your cream and season with 1 teaspoon of salt, then bring the mixture to a simmer and pop a lid on the pan. Cook for 7 minutes until the cream has thickened from the starch in the potatoes, and the potatoes are totally tender. Sprinkle in all but a handful of your remaining Cheddar, along with the spring onions. Season with 20 twists of black pepper, then give it a mix so it's all combined.

10   Spoon your potato mixture into the pastry case. Top with the last handful of Cheddar, then bake for 25 minutes. Remove from the oven and let it stand and set for 40 minutes, then remove it from the cake tin to slice and serve.

Brown Butter Cauliflower Risotto

Serves
4

Cook time
1 hour 20 minutes

1 small cauliflower

1 large onion

2 garlic cloves

bunch of sage

90g butter

350g risotto rice

150ml white wine

1.2 litres chicken or
vegetable stock

100g pecans

3 tbsp maple syrup

75g Parmesan or vegetarian
hard cheese

juice of 1 lemon

salt, pepper and olive oil

The cauliflower of my childhood evokes memories of something on the side of school dinners that may have resembled *cauliflower, but after one chew quickly became a mushy, pappy mess that tasted, dare I say it, a little bit farty. This may be the fate of boiled cauliflower, but roasting it is a whole other story. Getting a little bit of char on there lets those sugars caramelise, and gives you a distinctly nutty, grown-up flavour. I whizz it up here to form the base of this really quite autumnal risotto, finished with brown butter, crispy sage leaves and sweet pecans roasted in maple syrup. It is proper luxurious bowl food that you could make for someone in need of a treat.*

1 Preheat your oven to 210°C/190°C fan/gas mark 6½.

2 Chop your cauliflower into even-sized florets. Chop the leaves into pieces too, and the stalks.

3 Tip your cauliflower florets and stalks into a large baking tray, then drizzle them with 3 tablespoons of olive oil and ½ teaspoon of salt. Toss to combine, then roast for 30 minutes until the cauliflower is tender and starting to caramelise.

4 Meanwhile, peel and finely dice your onion. Peel and finely chop the garlic cloves. Finely chop about half of the sage, and pick the rest into leaves.

5 Melt 60g of your butter in a large sauté pan over a medium-low heat, and cook it until it has foamed up and is flecked with nutty pieces of brown. Tip your onion into the brown butter and cook gently for 15 minutes until softened. Add the garlic and chopped sage, then cook out for 2 minutes.

6 Once the cauliflower has been roasting for 30 minutes, add the cauliflower leaves to the same tray, then return to the oven and roast for another 10 minutes.

7 Add your risotto rice to the onion pan and lightly toast it in the butter for a few minutes, until the grains start to turn translucent. Pour in the white wine and give the mixture a stir.

8 Once your rice has absorbed the wine, gradually add your stock in small increments, stirring all the while to allow the rice grains to absorb the stock before the next addition. It should take about 25 minutes for all your stock to be added and for your rice to become tender.

continues overleaf

Brown Butter Cauliflower Risotto

9 While your rice cooks, tip all of your whole roasted cauliflower into a blender, along with 300ml water. Whizz to form a thick paste.

10 Meanwhile, reduce the oven temperature to 200°C/180°C fan/gas mark 6 and line a baking dish with baking parchment.

11 Roughly chop your pecans, then toss them in the prepared baking dish. Pour over your maple syrup and sprinkle with ¼ teaspoon of salt, then toss it all together to combine. Pop the dish in the oven for 15 minutes, stirring the pecans halfway through.

12 Melt your remaining 30g of butter in a saucepan over a medium heat, and add your whole sage leaves. Cook until the leaves are crispy and your butter has browned.

13 Stir the blitzed cauliflower into your risotto, and grate in all but a nubbin of your Parmesan. Squeeze in the lemon juice and give it a mix, then season to taste with salt and 15 twists of black pepper.

14 Spoon your risotto into bowls and top with your crispy sage leaves and butter, along with a grating of the remaining Parmesan and your maple pecans. Serve.

Sleepy Flatbreads

Makes
8 breads

Cook time
30 minutes,
plus overnight resting

1 tsp dried instant yeast

½ tsp caster sugar

450g strong white bread flour,
plus 30g for dusting

50g wholemeal flour

2 tsp fine sea salt

olive oil

These flatbreads get their name because there is nothing the dough loves more than a long snooze in the fridge. It gives the yeast time to slowly grow, giving you a lovely chewy texture and satisfying bubbles. People are often intimidated by making bread, but flatbread dough could not be simpler. You can throw it together really quickly, with the longest step being the rest time needed in the fridge. The longer you leave it, the more flavour you will get, as the yeast gets more time to have a little fermentation party. I would make the dough a night or two before you need it, and fry these breads off just before you are ready to serve.

1 Pour 300ml warm water into a large mixing bowl or stand mixer fitted with a dough hook attachment, then sprinkle in your yeast and sugar. Give it a whisk, then leave it to bubble up and bloom for 5 minutes.

2 Pour in both your flours and 2 tablespoons of the olive oil, then give your mixture a good stir so it is all combined. Tip in your salt at this point and mix again – salt kills yeast, so you want the flour to be fully incorporated to dilute the mixture before the salt is added.

3 Lightly flour your work surface, tip your shaggy dough out and knead for 5 minutes until you have a soft and springy dough.

4 Grease a medium-sized bowl with about 1 tablespoon of olive oil, then add your dough to the bowl. Tightly cover the top of the bowl with cling film, then place in the fridge. Leave it to sit for at least a few hours, but preferably overnight, by which time it should have doubled in size and become really bubbly.

5 When you are ready to cook your flatbreads, remove the dough from the fridge. Heat a cast-iron skillet or good-quality frying pan over a medium heat – you want it to gradually get quite hot.

6 Lightly oil your hands and the work surface with 1 tablespoon of olive oil. Tear off handfuls of dough – each portion should be about the size of a tangerine, or 100g. Use your hands to stretch each one and flatten into a circular shape about 2mm thick. It doesn't matter if it isn't perfectly round – I like them in all kinds of wibbly shapes.

7 Once the skillet is really hot, place your bread in the pan. Cook for about 2 minutes – the top should bubble up, and the base will get nice and golden. Flip and cook for another 2 minutes on the other side, then remove your bread from the pan and wrap it in a clean tea towel to keep it warm. Repeat with the remaining dough.

8 Serve them with whatever you like – they make most meals better.

Tip

They also freeze really well once cooked – just pop them into a Ziplock bag, and have bread ready in the freezer for months to come.

Cheesy Garlic Flatbreads

Makes
8

Cook time
15 minutes

3 garlic cloves

80g butter

small bunch of parsley

125g low-moisture mozzarella
(grated or a block will be fine)

1 portion of Sleepy Flatbread dough *(page 177; prepared up to step 4)*

30g Parmesan or vegetarian hard cheese

salt, pepper and olive oil

Is there a person on this earth who doesn't love garlic bread? Although I have a soft spot for the frozen multipack sticks you get in supermarkets, there is something really special about a fresh one made pizza-style. This uses the Sleepy Flatbreads dough on page 177 to make cheesy garlic bread that may well have people physically fighting across the table to get the last scrap. Don't say I didn't warn you.

1 Preheat your grill to high. Heat a cast-iron skillet or ovenproof frying pan over a medium heat – you want it to gradually become quite hot.

2 Peel and finely chop your garlic, then place it in a bowl with your butter. Pop this in the microwave for 30 seconds to melt, or simply melt it in a small saucepan over a low heat.

3 Finely chop your parsley, then stir this into the melted butter. Chop your mozzarella into small pieces.

4 Remove your dough from the fridge. Lightly oil your hands and the work surface with 1 tablespoon of olive oil. Tear off handfuls of dough – each one should be about the size of a tangerine, or 100g. Use your hands to stretch each one out and flatten it into a circular shape about 2mm thick, with a slightly raised border around the edge. It doesn't matter if it isn't perfectly round – in fact, I like them in all kinds of wibbly shapes. Repeat with the remaining dough.

5 Place the first bread into your skillet. Cook for about 2 minutes – the surface should bubble up, and start to visibly dry out, while the base should be golden. Sprinkle the surface of the bread with some of the mozzarella, then remove the pan from the hob and place it under the grill. Grill for about 2 minutes, until the cheese has melted and the bread has puffed up and gone golden.

6 Remove the flatbread from the pan, then brush with your garlic butter. Grate over a little Parmesan, then top with a pinch of flaky sea salt and a few cracks of black pepper. Keep it warm and repeat with the remaining dough and cheese to make the rest of your flatbreads. Serve.

Potatoes for Mum

Serves
4

Cook time
30 minutes

1kg baby potatoes

140g butter

½ small bunch of chives

2 tsp yeast extract
(I use Marmite)

50g Cheddar *(optional)*

salt and olive oil

My mum essentially lives off Marmite on toast and Twiglets, so my body is quite literally built from the stuff. I still turn to the savoury spread for my subsistence, and also for the purest form of comfort. An old Nigella recipe that has got me through more hangovers and low periods than I can count is her Marmite pasta. I discovered not long ago that Marmite butter potatoes are a similarly incredible thing, that I could quite easily just sit and demolish on the sofa as a meal in of themselves. So this recipe is for my mum, and my honorary TV mum, both of whom are my biggest food inspirations. The Marmite isn't too overbearing, so these still make a really nice side for a bit of chicken or white fish without taking the accompaniment over too much. It just lends a bit of umami punch, which is always very welcome to me.

1 Halve your potatoes lengthways, then place them in a medium-sized saucepan. Pour over boiling water to cover and season with salt, then place over a medium-high heat and bring to the boil. Once boiling, reduce the heat to low and simmer for 10 minutes.

2 Meanwhile, cut your butter into cubes, and finely dice your chives.

3 Preheat your grill to high. Once your potatoes are tender, drain them in a colander, then leave them to steam dry for a couple of minutes.

4 Tip your potatoes onto a baking tray, and drizzle over 2 tablespoons of olive oil. Toss to coat, then place them under the grill. Grill for 5–10 minutes, depending on how hot your grill runs, flipping them over halfway through until they are lightly blistered (but they won't be totally crispy).

5 Place your original potato saucepan over a low heat and add 90ml water. Once it is hot, add your butter, a cube at a time, whisking until it has melted and emulsified before adding the next cube. Spoon in your yeast extract, and give it one last whisk to combine.

6 Pour the buttery sauce over the potatoes, and sprinkle over the chives. Grate over 50g Cheddar at the end too, if you are feeling extra. Serve.

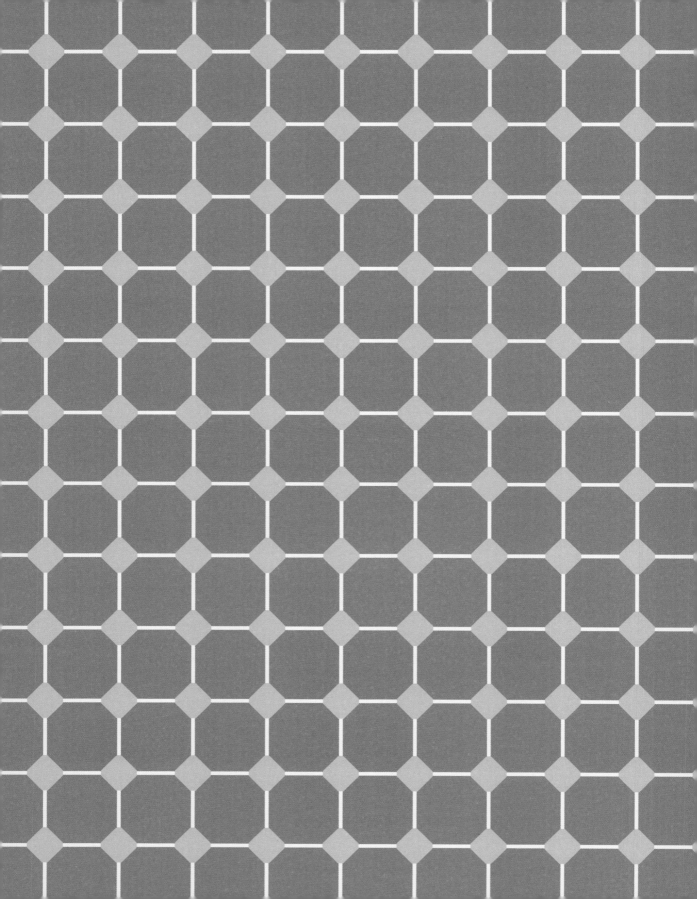

Veg Me Up

I absolutely love that lots of dinners these days involve many, many delicious vegetable dishes, served up in a group to create a big omnivorous feast. I crave vegetables frequently, and you will often find me eating a great pile of them for dinner after an indulgent eating period. This chapter is made up of salads for warmer seasons and roasted veg for cooler ones, to scratch the itch if you too like eating this way. You can serve lots together as a big ensemble party, but most of them are also substantial enough to be the main event of a meal. This is undoubtedly the most vibrant, kaleidoscopic chapter in this book, with a rainbow of veg from across the seasons being championed in different ways to create some quite fabulous things to tuck into.

Sticky Tamarind Carrots with Green Chilli Yoghurt

Serves
4

Cook time
1 hour

500g heritage carrots
(with their tops on)

1 tsp ground cumin

½ tsp kashmiri chilli powder
(or mild chilli powder)

juice of 1 lemon

bunch of mint

3 green chillies

350g coconut yoghurt or thick natural yoghurt

1 garlic clove

400g tin of chickpeas

6 tbsp tamarind sauce
(I like the Maggi one)

flatbreads, *to serve (optional)*

salt, pepper and olive oil

Roasted carrots are a top-tier vegetable. A trip to a scorching location (the oven) with a drizzle of oil turns them into something gnarly and witchy-looking, with a rich, caramelised flavour. It is without a shadow of a doubt my favourite way to eat them, and I've cooked versions of this dish more times than I can count. I would go so far to say that it has become one of my personality traits. If you are coming round for a big dinner spread at mine, you better believe that I will be sneaking some form of sticky roasted carrot onto your plate. This version makes a great side for a roast dinner, barbecue or curry, but is equally satisfying as a stand-alone meal with bread to serve.

1   Preheat your oven to 210°C/190°C fan/gas mark 6½.

2   Trim the green tops off your carrots and save these for later. Tip the carrots into a roasting tray and drizzle them with 2 tablespoons of olive oil, then scatter over your cumin and chilli powder, as well as 1 teaspoon of salt and 10 grinds of black pepper. Shake the tray so that the carrots are totally coated in the spices and oil, then roast for 30 minutes.

3   Meanwhile, finely chop a handful of your carrot tops until you have about 2 tablespoons' worth. Using a pestle and mortar, bash the carrot tops along with the lemon juice and 2 tablespoons of olive oil, until you have a chunky green sauce.

4   Finely chop the mint and green chillies. Spoon your yoghurt into a bowl, then grate in the garlic and add your mint and chillies. Add ½ teaspoon of salt, then give the whole thing a mix until combined.

5   When the carrots have been roasting for 30 minutes, drain your chickpeas and give them a rinse, then toss them onto the roasting tray. Return to the oven for 15 minutes until the chickpeas are crisp.

6   When everything is ready, remove your carrots and chickpeas from the oven. Pour the tamarind sauce over the top, and give them a toss until they are all coated.

7   Spoon your yoghurt onto a serving plate and top it with your chickpeas and carrots. Drizzle with the carrot top oil, then serve and enjoy with bread for dipping.

Charred Cauliflower with Prosciutto and Almonds

Serves
4

Cook time
1 hour

2 small cauliflowers

200g baby onions

7 tbsp sherry vinegar

4 tbsp caster sugar

140g prosciutto

110g blanched almonds

60g white bread

1 garlic clove

small handful of parsley leaves

salt, pepper and olive oil

Tip

I love the crunchy shards of prosciutto in here, but you could leave them out for the veggie squad.

Platters of roasted veg with a sea of creamy sauce swooshed beneath them are nothing new, but it is a stunning way to serve them, so here I go again. The creamy sauce here is a thick ajo blanco, a creamy almond sauce rich with sherry vinegar and garlic, and it is rather lovely with nutty roasted cauliflower, jammy little onions and crisp, salty prosciutto.

1 Preheat your oven to 210°C/190°C fan/gas mark 6½.

2 Trim the leaves off your cauliflowers, then cut the cauliflower heads into quarters, so that you have 8 equal-sized wedges. Rub the wedges with 1 teaspoon of salt and 2 tablespoons of olive oil.

3 Heat a large frying pan over a medium heat. Working in batches, add a few of the cauliflower wedges at a time, placing them in the frying pan cut-side down. Pan-fry for about 2 minutes on each cut side until they have a nice golden crust, then remove from the pan and repeat with the remaining wedges. Arrange them cut-sides up on a large baking tray, and roast for 25 minutes.

4 Meanwhile, peel your baby onions, leaving them whole. Heat 2 tablespoons of olive oil in a large sauté pan over a medium heat. Add the onions and fry for about 3 minutes until lightly golden. Add 4 tablespoons of the sherry vinegar, along with the sugar and 150ml water, then cover the pan with a lid. Reduce the heat to low and leave to simmer for 20 minutes, adding another splash of water if it looks like it is drying out.

5 Once your cauliflower wedges have been roasting for 25 minutes, remove the baking tray from the oven and add the prosciutto slices. Return to the oven for 5 minutes, then flip over the prosciutto and roast for another 5 minutes. They should get really crispy.

6 Meanwhile, make your almond sauce. Tip your blanched almonds into a dry frying pan over a medium heat and toast them for 3 minutes, or until they are lightly golden. Cut your bread into small cubes, and peel and smash the garlic clove.

7 Add 90g of the almonds to a blender, along with the bread, garlic and remaining 3 tablespoons of sherry vinegar. Add 6 tablespoons of olive oil and 200ml water, then whizz it all up until you have a really smooth, thick sauce. You may need to scrape down the sides of the blender to get it to this stage. Season to taste with salt.

8 Swoosh your almond sauce across the base of a platter. Arrange the cauliflower wedges, onions and prosciutto on top, then drizzle over any extra onion juices. Roughly chop the remaining almonds and sprinkle on top along with the parsley leaves before serving.

Marinated Pepper Couscous with Feta

Serves
4

Cook time
40 minutes, plus marinating

6 Romano peppers

1 garlic clove

½ small bunch of parsley

juice of 1 lemon

2 tsp sherry vinegar

1 tsp Aleppo chilli flakes
(or sweet smoked paprika)

300g giant couscous

30g sourdough bread

1 tbsp coriander seeds

100g feta

salt and olive oil

Tip
This will keep in the fridge for up to 3 days with its elements separated, so it's excellent for meal prep.

There is something very graceful and majestic about the pointiness of Romano peppers. They are sweeter than chunky bell peppers, and their skins are more delicate, making it less faff to peel them after charring the peppers under a grill. This dish would be ideal to bring to a barbecue or summery dinner, either as a side or as the main event.

1 Preheat your grill to high. Place your Romano peppers on a baking tray and drizzle with 1 tablespoon of olive oil. Place under the grill for about 10 minutes, turning over halfway so they cook evenly.

2 Meanwhile, peel and very finely chop your garlic, and roughly chop all but a few leaves of your parsley.

3 Remove your pepper tray from the grill and place a tea towel over the top. This will steam them as they cool, to get them even softer.

4 When your peppers are just cool enough to handle, peel off their skins. Tear the flesh open and discard the seeds, then tear the flesh into strips and add to a large mixing bowl. Add 8 tablespoons of olive oil, as well as the garlic, chopped parsley, lemon juice, sherry vinegar, Aleppo chilli flakes and 1 teaspoon of salt. Give it a stir, then leave to marinate at room temperature for at least an hour. If you could do this bit a few days in advance, even better!

5 Heat a sauté pan over a medium heat. Add the couscous and toast for about 3 minutes in the dry pan until the grains are slightly golden.

6 Pour in as much boiling water as if you were cooking pasta, and season with 1 tablespoon of salt. Simmer for 7 minutes, until your couscous is tender, then drain in a colander.

7 Meanwhile, make your sourdough crumbs. Cut the bread into small pieces, add it to a food processor and pulse into chunky crumbs.

8 Toast the coriander seeds in a small frying pan over a medium heat for 2 minutes until they are fragrant. Using a pestle and mortar, give them a gentle bash to break them down.

9 Add 2 tablespoons of olive oil to the same frying pan over a medium heat. Tip in your breadcrumbs and toast for 3 minutes, or until each piece is golden. Tip these into a bowl with your bashed coriander seeds, then add ½ teaspoon of salt and give it all a mix.

10 Tip your drained couscous into the bowl with the peppers, and give it all a mix. Crumble the feta on top in big chunks and stir through.

11 Spoon the couscous on to the base of a serving plate. Top with your crispy breadcrumbs and the remaining parsley leaves, then serve.

Crispy Tofu, Grapefruit and Peanut Salad

Serves
4

Cook time
45 minutes

300g firm tofu

2½ tbsp cornflour

2 shallots

600g medium-sized tomatoes
on the vine

2 grapefruits *(white or
pink is fine)*

1 red chilli

zest and juice of 2 limes

2 tbsp sesame oil

1 tsp caster sugar

100g salted peanuts

small bunch of coriander

small bunch of mint

salt, pepper and vegetable oil

There are many people out there who are averse to fruit in savoury things. While I can understand how somebody could find a surprise burst of sweetness from a dried apricot in a tagine troubling, I do not think the same can be said for citrus fruit in salads. The brightness of an orange segment is lovely, but what I like even more are the grown-up, bitter notes that grapefruit brings to the table. It adds something really special to this summery salad, and works a treat with the crispy, peppery tofu, sweet tomatoes and crispy herbs. By all means, whack some rice noodles in here too for a more substantial meal, but I really enjoy this as a lighter one.

1   Preheat your oven to 220°C/200°C fan/gas mark 7.

2   Drain your tofu, then cut it into 2cm cubes. Add your cornflour to a medium-sized bowl, along with 15 twists of black pepper and 1 teaspoon of salt. Give it a mix so it is all combined, then add your tofu. Toss the tofu in the seasoned flour so that it is evenly coated.

3   Arrange the tofu on a baking tray, and drizzle over 2 tablespoons of vegetable oil. Bake for 30 minutes, turning the tofu over halfway through so that it crisps up evenly.

4   Meanwhile, peel your shallots, then very finely slice them into rounds. Cut your tomatoes into chunks. Set a sieve over a bowl, and add your tomatoes and shallots to it. Add 1 teaspoon of salt, then give them a mix and leave them to sit. This will draw out the excess moisture and season them.

5   Cut the rind off your grapefruits with a little serrated knife, then slice the flesh into rounds.

6   To make your dressing, finely chop the chilli, then add this to the liquid from the tomatoes. Add the lime zest and juice, along with the sesame oil and sugar, then give it a whisk to combine.

7   Using a pestle and mortar, give your peanuts a bash to break them up. You don't want a fine powder, just coarse pieces.

8   Pick the leaves off your coriander and mint.

9   Heat 2 tablespoons of vegetable oil in a frying pan over a medium heat. Add the mint leaves and fry for 30 seconds until they turn translucent, then lift them out of the oil with a slotted spoon. Place them on a plate lined with paper towels to drain and crisp up a bit.

10 In a large bowl, combine the tomatoes, grapefruit, tofu, coriander and half of your peanuts. Pour over the dressing and toss everything together. Scoop the salad onto a platter, then top it with your crispy mint leaves and remaining peanuts. Serve.

Double Sprout, Blue Cheese and Cranberry Salad

Serves
4

Cook time
40 minutes

1kg Brussels sprouts

1 red onion

juice of ½ lemon

100g blanched hazelnuts

100g dried cranberries

150g blue cheese (*I use Stilton for its crumbliness*)

For the dressing
2 tsp brown rice miso paste

3 tbsp Dijon mustard

2 tsp apple cider vinegar

½ tsp caster sugar

salt, pepper and olive oil

I'm glad we are in the era where Brussels sprouts are getting recognised as the babes that they are. The boiled, squishy versions that sullied their name in the last century are fading from our memories, and we have learned to embrace eating them with a bit of texture. This salad is inspired by one I ate in New York at Emily, a cute West Village spot famed for its Detroit-style pizzas and burgers. While both the burgers and pizzas were lovely, the part we still talk about is the salad: a heap of shredded sprouts with blue cheese, dried cherries and a really savoury dressing. I've added roasted sprouts and hazelnuts for an extra flavour bomb.

1 Preheat your oven to 220°C/200°C fan/gas mark 7.

2 Trim the ends off half of your sprouts, then halve them lengthways.

3 Drizzle a baking tray with 1 tablespoon of olive oil, and spread it all over the tray. Place your sprouts on the tray, cut-sides down, then drizzle over another tablespoon of olive oil. Sprinkle with ½ teaspoon of salt, then bake for 25 minutes until crisp and golden.

4 Meanwhile, peel and finely slice your red onion and pop it into a bowl. Squeeze over the lemon juice, then add a pinch of salt. Scrunch it all up with your hands to start pickling, then set aside.

5 Very finely shred the rest of your sprouts with a sharp knife – the finer the better. You could use a mandolin, but I find it a bit faffy with a vegetable this small.

6 Tip your shredded sprouts into a bowl with ½ teaspoon of salt. Massage with your hands for a few minutes to soften the sprouts.

7 When the sprouts in the oven still have 5 minutes left to cook, tip your hazelnuts onto a separate baking tray and pop these into the oven to toast for the last 5 minutes.

8 To make your dressing, dilute your miso paste with 1 tablespoon of hot water in a small bowl. Add the Dijon mustard, apple cider vinegar and sugar, along with 6 tablespoons of olive oil. Season to taste with salt and a good few grinds of black pepper, then whisk it up with a fork to make a dressing.

9 Roughly chop your roasted hazelnuts – you still want some big chunks in there. Tip your roasted sprouts into the large bowl of shredded sprouts. Add the drained pickled red onions, chopped hazelnuts and dried cranberries. Crumble in 120g of the blue cheese, then add the dressing. Give the salad a really good toss.

10 Scoop it onto a serving dish, and top with more crumbled blue cheese. Serve it up as a wintry side salad, or as a meal in itself.

Charred Broccoli and Curried Lentil Salad

Serves
4

Cook time
1 hour

2 onions

3 garlic cloves

1 tsp coriander seeds

1 tsp cumin seeds

2 tbsp tomato purée

2 tbsp curry powder

½ tsp ground turmeric

½ tsp kashmiri chilli powder
(or mild chilli powder)

300g dried Puy lentils

400g Tenderstem broccoli

150g thick natural yoghurt

juice of ½ lime, *plus wedges
to serve*

salt, pepper, olive oil
and vegetable oil

A big picky summer spread holds a very special place in my heart. On summer holidays in France when I was growing up, we would shimmy across from our poolside perch to a table in the shade, littered with a vast array of cheeses, cold cuts, rillettes, pickles and bread. The highlights for me were the occasional rotisserie chicken that would find its way there (still a thing that makes me weak at the knees), and a lentil salad my mum used to put together, which has very much inspired this dish. She would simmer the Puy lentils in an oniony stock flecked with spices; in this recipe, I sneak some of the spiced onions from the pan before you cook the lentils to provide a sweet and spicy hit for the yoghurt topping. This is great eaten warm, but will also keep for a few days in the fridge, providing you with a nourishing lunch for days on end.

1   Preheat your oven to 220°C/200°C fan/gas mark 7.

2   Peel, halve and finely chop one of your onions. Peel and finely chop your garlic too.

3   Heat a large saucepan over a medium heat. Add your coriander seeds and cumin seeds, and toast for about 2 minutes until they are fragrant. Remove them from the pan and lightly crush using a pestle and mortar, to break them down a bit.

4   Add 4 tablespoons of olive oil to the same saucepan. Tip your chopped onion into the pan, along with a little pinch of salt, and cook for 15–20 minutes until softened, adding an occasional splash of water if it looks like it is at risk of burning.

5   Meanwhile, peel and finely slice your remaining onion. Heat 6 tablespoons of vegetable oil in a separate frying pan, adding your sliced onion while the pan is still warming up. Fry for about 5 minutes until the onion slices have turned golden. Remove them from the pan with a slotted spoon, and pop them on a plate lined with paper towels to cool and crisp up.

6   Add your toasted spices, garlic, tomato purée, curry powder, turmeric and chilli powder to the pan with the chopped onions. Cook these out for 2 minutes, or until fragrant.

7   Tip your Puy lentils into a sieve and rinse with cold water for about 30 seconds.

continues overleaf

Charred Broccoli and Curried Lentil Salad

8 Remove 2 tablespoons of the spiced onion mixture from the pan and set aside, then tip your rinsed Puy lentils into the pan. Add 900ml water and bring to the boil, then reduce the heat to low and leave to simmer for 25 minutes.

9 Add your broccoli to a large baking tray, and drizzle it with 2 tablespoons of olive oil. Season with ½ teaspoon of salt and toss to coat, then roast in the oven for 10 minutes.

10 Meanwhile, spoon the reserved 2 tablespoons of spiced onion mixture into a pestle and mortar, and bash it to a smooth paste. Add the yoghurt and lime juice, then stir to combine. Season to taste with salt.

11 Once your lentils have cooked, season them to taste with salt, and leave to cool for 10 minutes. They should have absorbed most of their liquid at this point. When you're ready to serve, tip them into a large bowl and add the broccoli. Toss to combine.

12 Spoon your broccoli and lentils on to a serving platter, then spoon over the curry yoghurt. Sprinkle over the crispy onions, then serve with lime wedges for squeezing.

All the Greens, Apple and Ginger Salad

Serves
6

Cook time
30 minutes, plus cooling

125g cashews

200g sugar snap peas

150g frozen edamame beans

200g Tenderstem broccoli

½ hispi cabbage

1 apple

½ small bunch of coriander

For the dressing
3cm knob of ginger

1 red chilli

4 tbsp light soy sauce

juice of 1 lime

½ tsp caster sugar

salt and sesame oil

Pictured on page 198

In the summer, my mum makes a classic salad packed with verdant, crisp vegetables with a zingy lime and chilli dressing. I knew that I needed to put my own version of this iconic Wyburd family salad in this book, so here she is. I was also inspired by a little M&S one that I often pick up for a train picnic (alongside a prawn sandwich, sausage rolls, crisps and fruit, of course – I'm not that *boring), which has the sweet crunch of apple running through it. I tried putting garlic in this dressing when I first tested it, only to be reminded that garlic and apple are a distinctly weird combination. Instead, fiery ginger, chilli and lime do the legwork to make this dressing a hit.*

1   Preheat your oven to 180°C/160°C fan/gas mark 4.

2   Tip the cashews onto a baking tray and bake for 12 minutes until they are golden. Leave them on the tray to cool.

3   Bring a large pan of lightly salted water to the boil. Once it is there, tip in your sugar snaps, edamame and broccoli. Simmer for 3 minutes.

4   While the veg cooks, fill a large bowl with cold water and ice. Once the 3 minutes are up, drain the veg in a colander, then tip straight into the iced water. Allow the veg to cool completely, then remove from the water and set aside to dry. This process will keep them bright green and crisp.

5   To make your dressing, finely chop the ginger and chilli, then add these to a small bowl. Add the soy sauce and lime juice, along with 2 tablespoons of sesame oil and the caster sugar, then give it all a good mix. Season to taste with salt.

6   Prep the rest of your veg for the salad. Finely shred your cabbage, then peel your apple and finely slice it too (if you aren't eating for a while, submerge the apple slices in a bowl of water with a little lime juice – this will stop them from browning). Pick your coriander leaves.

7   Tip the cabbage into a large bowl. Season with ½ teaspoon of salt, and lightly massage with your fingers for a minute to soften it slightly. Add the rest of your prepped veg to the bowl, along with the apple, cashews and coriander leaves. Pour in the dressing, and give it all a good toss.

8   Scoop your salad onto a platter and serve.

Anchovy and Parmesan Courgette Salad

Serves
4

Cook time
50 minutes

3 courgettes

juice of 1 lemon

100g sourdough bread

2 baby gem lettuces

small bunch of chives

1 egg yolk

1 garlic clove

4 anchovies

2 tbsp white wine vinegar

½ tsp Dijon mustard

50g Parmesan

salt, pepper and olive oil

Tip
You may have a little dressing left over – this will keep in the fridge, covered, for 2 days.

As a society, we brush things off as being 'basic' too readily. Lots of the things tarnished with the 'basic' brush – burrata, Aperol spritz, iced coffees – are popular because they are so great. Caesar salad is no exception. It has the most indulgent and delicious salad dressing out there, and deserves all the praise it gets. This salad is Caesar-esque, as I think anchovies and courgettes get along like a house on fire. I'm very into using courgettes two ways in salads – in chunks, fried hard to get a lovely char, and raw, very finely sliced on a mandolin. This makes a brilliant side salad, though I would also very happily eat it alone for my lunch or dinner.

1 Preheat your oven to 200°C/180°C fan/gas mark 6.

2 Chop 2 of your courgettes into irregular chunks on the diagonal, about 3cm thick at their thickest part. Tip these into a bowl, and toss with half the lemon juice, 1 tablespoon of olive oil and 1 teaspoon of salt.

3 Heat a large frying pan over a high heat. Add the courgette chunks and fry them really hard for a few minutes, so they get a nice caramelised colour on all sides but aren't falling apart. Set them aside until later.

4 To make the croutons, tear your bread into bite-sized pieces, then pop onto a baking tray. Drizzle with 1 tablespoon of olive oil and give them a good toss to coat. Pop the tray into the oven for 10 minutes.

5 Finely slice your remaining courgette using a mandolin. Trim the ends off your baby gem, and separate out the leaves. Toss the courgette rounds and lettuce leaves in a large mixing bowl. Finely chop your chives.

6 Add your egg yolk to a blender. Peel the garlic clove, then grate it in. Add the anchovies, white wine vinegar, Dijon mustard and remaining lemon juice, along with 6 tablespoons of olive oil and 4 tablespoons of water. Grate in 45g of your Parmesan, then season your dressing to taste with salt and 20 twists of black pepper. Whizz it up to combine into a thick dressing.

7 Add your grilled courgettes to your salad bowl, as well as all but a handful of your chives. Pour the dressing over the top and toss with your hands so that all the veg gets coated in dressing. Get your croutons in there, and toss it again.

8 Spoon the salad onto a serving plate, and grate over the remaining Parmesan. Sprinkle on the remaining chives and serve.

Beetroot, Burrata and Curry Leaf Salad

Serves
2

Cook time
30 minutes

300g raw candy beetroots
*(you could use regular raw
beetroot if you like, but candy
beetroot is a lot more aesthetically
pleasing if you can seek it out)*

juice of 2 limes

250g cooked beetroot

1 shallot

4 garlic cloves

1 red chilli

1 tsp cumin seeds

½ tsp black mustard seeds

bunch of fresh curry leaves

2 tbsp rice wine vinegar

¼ tsp caster sugar

1 burrata

salt, pepper and rapeseed oil

Beetroots are a vegetable that some people struggle to get excited about. Rich, sweet and earthy, admittedly even I can go off them halfway through a plate of food – sometimes they're just a bit much. However, I'm glad to report that I have discovered the optimum way to enjoy them: match them with something fatty and creamy, and big bold flavours that hit you across the face as you eat. Enter this curry leaf, crispy garlic and chilli dressing, rich with lime to cut through the sweetness, with soft burrata oozing over the top. I'm going to put it out there and say this is the most beautiful recipe in the book.

1   Start by prepping your beetroot. Peel your candy beetroots, then slice very finely on a mandolin. You could do this with a sharp knife if you didn't have a mandolin, but you want them to be sliced as finely as possible. Place these slices in a large bowl, and squeeze over the juice of 1 lime.

2   Chop your cooked beetroot into pieces. Peel and finely slice your shallot and garlic. Finely slice your chilli.

3   Heat about 5 tablespoons of rapeseed oil in a frying pan over a medium heat. Add your shallots while the oil is still heating up, and fry for about 3 minutes until they just start to take on colour. At this stage, add your garlic, chilli, cumin seeds, mustard seeds and curry leaves. Cook for another 2 minutes until the seeds pop and the garlic is just starting to turn golden. Scoop the crispy bits out of the pan with a slotted spoon, and leave them on a plate lined with paper towels to cool and crisp up.

4   Tip the oil into a heatproof bowl and allow it to cool. Add your rice wine vinegar and squeeze in the remaining lime juice. Add the sugar and season the dressing to taste with salt.

5   Add your cooked beetroot to the bowl of raw beetroot slices. Pour over most of the dressing, and give it all a toss to combine.

6   Arrange your beetroots on a plate, then tear open the burrata and place it on top. Sprinkle over the crispy shallots and curry leaf mixture, then pour over any extra dressing and serve.

Bitter Leaves with Butter Bean Croutons

Serves
6 as a side

Cook time
40 minutes

2 × 400g tins of butter beans

4 rosemary sprigs

6 garlic cloves

4 red endives or 1 large radicchio

2 baby gem lettuces

1 red onion

juice of 2 lemons

2 tsp Dijon mustard

6 tbsp red wine vinegar

salt, pepper and olive oil

Side salads do not have to be a limp and boring affair. I often use 'a crisp salad' as a description for a side dish suggestion, and I am firmly of the belief that the dressing has to be pretty punchy. The bitterness of endive is an absolute joy here, offset by the mustardy dressing, sweet with roasted garlic. The star of the show, though, is the crispy butter beans, who have rubbed shoulders with olive oil and rosemary during a short spell in the oven, adding texture and bulk to this dish. In fact, the addition of the beans makes this feel substantial and exciting enough that you may very well promote it from side dish to main.

1 Preheat your oven to 200°C/180°C fan/gas mark 6.

2 Drain your butter beans, then rinse them with water. Pat them dry with paper towels, then tip them into a baking tray. Pick the rosemary leaves into the tin, then add your whole garlic cloves, skins and all. Drizzle with 4 tablespoons of olive oil and season with ½ teaspoon of salt, then toss it all around so the beans are coated in oil. Bake for 20–25 minutes, until crispy and golden.

3 Meanwhile, cut the ends off your endives or radicchio and baby gem lettuces and separate out the leaves. You may need to occasionally trim down more of the ends to release more leaves. Pop these in a colander and give them a rinse with cold water, then set aside.

4 Peel and finely slice your red onion, then pop this into a small bowl. Squeeze over the lemon juice and ½ teaspoon of salt, and scrunch it up with your hands to start pickling the onion.

5 Squeeze your roasted garlic cloves out of their skins and into a small bowl. Add the Dijon mustard, red wine vinegar and 12 tablespoons of olive oil to the bowl, then season your dressing to taste with salt and 10 twists of black pepper. Whisk to combine.

6 Add your leaves to a salad bowl and pour over the roasted garlic dressing. Briefly massage the dressing into the leaves so that each leaf is coated, then add the pickled onions and roasted butter beans. Toss the salad so all the ingredients are combined, then serve.

Pistachio Pesto Chickpeas with Stracciatella

Serves
4

Cook time
20 minutes, plus chilling

125g mozzarella ball

70ml double cream

50g pistachio kernels

2 small bunches of basil

1 small garlic clove

40g Parmesan or vegetarian
hard cheese

60ml olive oil

juice of 1 lemon

1 large posh jar of chickpeas
(or 2 × 400g tins)

salt, pepper and olive oil

When we talk about stracciatella, we are talking about one of two things. It is a creamy, chocolate-flecked ice cream that my Grunk (our name for my dad's dad) used to give me as a child in the summer, but it is also the liquid-gold gooey stuff you'd find inside a ball of burrata. The latter is traditionally made by mixing fresh mozzarella curds with thick cream, but I learned from the brilliant cook and recipe developer Claire Thomson that you can make a cheat's version by mixing crème fraîche with shredded mozzarella. I gave it a go with double cream and, let me tell you, it is magical. *It is delicious on pretty much anything, but here I blob it on top of chickpeas tossed with a herby pistachio pesto. This would be phenomenal as a DIY sandwich filling to bring to a picnic, or as a cute little summery side.*

1   Drain your mozzarella, then tear it into small pieces. Place it in a bowl, then pour in your double cream. Give it a mix, then cover and set it aside at room temperature for an hour. Something magical will happen: the mozzarella and cream will start to coagulate, creating stringy stracciatella.

2   Meanwhile, make your pesto. Toast your pistachio kernels in a dry frying pan over a medium heat for 2 minutes until they are lightly toasted. Allow them to cool slightly, then tip into a food processor.

3   Add the basil to the food processor, stalks and all, setting aside a few leaves for later. Bash your garlic clove to remove the skin, then add that, too. Grate in your Parmesan, then whizz together, slowly drizzling in 60ml of olive oil as you go. You should have a vibrant green sauce. Add the lemon juice, then season your pesto to taste with salt and 10 twists of black pepper.

4   Drain your chickpeas, then give them a rinse. Pat them dry with paper towels, then tip them into a bowl. Pour in your pesto and mix so that the pesto totally dresses the chickpeas, but be gentle – you don't want the chickpeas to break down.

5   When you are ready to eat, divide the chickpeas between plates and spoon your stracciatella over the top. Twist over some black pepper, add the reserved basil leaves and drizzle with a little olive oil to serve.

Baked Feta with Honey Harissa Aubergines

Serves
4

Cook time
1 hour

1 red pepper

2 aubergines

3 garlic cloves

1 tsp ground cinnamon

1 tsp hot smoked paprika

400g tinned chopped tomatoes

2 tbsp rose harissa paste

2 tbsp honey

200g block of feta

¼ small bunch of basil

¼ small bunch of parsley
(optional)

pittas or flatbreads, *to serve*
(optional)

salt, pepper and olive oil

Spicy and sweet flavour combinations will never cease to fill me with joy, and one of the best iterations of this partnership is honey and harissa paste. Get your paws on some rose harissa for this – they sell it in most big supermarkets. The floral notes add something extra special. The whole block of feta nestled into the middle of the sticky veg turns soft and jelly-like when baked, and it is a dream to scoop up with flatbreads. I love this as a one-pan dinner in and of itself, but it would also be amazing as part of a larger spread.

1   Preheat your oven to 220°C/200°C fan/gas mark 7.

2   Finely slice your pepper into 5cm long batons. Cut your aubergines into 4cm chunks. Peel and finely chop your garlic.

3   Heat 2 tablespoons of olive oil in a medium-sized ovenproof frying pan or skillet. Tip in half of your aubergine batons and fry for about 7 minutes until they are super soft and collapsing. Remove from the pan and repeat with the remaining aubergine batons, then set aside.

4   Add another 3 tablespoons of olive oil to the same pan, then tip in your sliced pepper. Cook for 5 minutes with a pinch of salt until totally softened, then add your garlic, cinnamon and paprika. Cook for 2 minutes.

5   Return the aubergines to the pan, then stir in the chopped tomatoes, rose harissa and honey. Bring the whole mixture to a simmer, then season to taste with salt. Remove from the heat.

6   Create a well in the middle of the pan, then pop your block of feta into it. Drizzle the top of the feta with 1 tablespoon of olive oil, then place the pan in the oven for 20 minutes to bake.

7   Preheat your grill to high, then remove the pan from the oven and grill for 2 minutes, or until the feta gets a golden top. Keep a close eye on it – you don't want the veg to burn.

8   Pick the leaves from the basil and the parsley, if using, then scatter over the top. Serve with bread for dunking.

Sizzly Leek Vinaigrette with Green Yoghurt Beans

Serves
4

Cook time
45 minutes

4 leeks

400ml vegetable stock

2 tbsp red wine vinegar

1 tbsp Dijon mustard

½ tsp caster sugar

1 garlic clove

small bunch of mint

200g thick natural yoghurt

small bunch of parsley

zest and juice of ½ lemon

1 large posh jar of cannellini beans (*or 2 × 400g tins*)

1 tsp Aleppo chilli flakes

salt, pepper and olive oil

There are a few things that make this recipe great: the sweet-and-sour braised leeks; the beans tossed in the most heavenly yoghurt-y, herby sauce reminiscent of a green goddess dressing; the herbs crisped up in Aleppo chilli oil. Box it up to take with you on a summery excursion and you will be the most beloved person at the party. Serve it to your family as part of a big summer feast, and you will probably become your granny's favourite. It occupies the sweet spot of feeling light and healthy, but also indulgent at the same time.

1   Cut your leeks into cylinders about 4cm tall. Arrange them tightly in a small, high-sided skillet or sauté pan, so that they fill all the space, then pour over your vegetable stock and 1 tablespoon of the red wine vinegar. Place the pan over a medium heat and bring to a simmer, then reduce the heat to low and place a circle of baking parchment on top. Simmer for 20 minutes until the leeks are tender, then allow to cool.

2   While your leeks simmer, move on to your vinaigrette. Add the remaining 1 tablespoon of red wine vinegar to a bowl, along with the mustard and sugar. Season to taste with salt, add 3 tablespoons of olive oil, then whisk it all to combine.

3   To make your green yoghurt, peel your garlic clove and pick your mint leaves. Tip the yoghurt into a blender, along with the parsley (stalks and all), half the mint leaves, your garlic clove and the lemon zest and juice. Whizz it all up to create a vibrant green sauce, then season to taste with salt.

4   Once your leeks have cooled a little, carefully remove them from their braising liquid – you want them to stay in solid little barrels rather than falling apart. Pop them on a plate and spoon over your vinaigrette. Let them sit for a bit to soak up the flavours.

5   Drain your beans and give them a rinse, then add to a mixing bowl. Pour over your green yoghurt, then give it a good mix to combine.

6   Spoon the beans onto a serving plate, then top them with the leek vinaigrette.

7   Heat 4 tablespoons of olive oil in a small frying pan over a medium heat, then drop in the remaining mint leaves. Fry for about 30 seconds until the leaves have turned a little translucent, then add the Aleppo chilli flakes. Spoon this spicy, herby oil all over your leeks and serve.

Sesame Caponata

Serves
6

Cook time
1 hour

2 red peppers

3 aubergines

2 celery sticks

2 red onions

400g tinned chopped tomatoes

3 tbsp red wine vinegar

1 tsp caster sugar

50g capers

80g sultanas

3 tbsp tahini

2 tbsp toasted sesame seeds

salt, pepper and olive oil

As the London weather gets increasingly spicy in the summertime, I find myself wanting to cook as little as possible. Meals you can prep and keep in the fridge for days at a time, to be portioned out by weary hands after a traumatic 40-degree tube journey, are nothing short of a godsend. Caponata is one of the best versions of this concept: fried-up veg, flavoured and preserved with sugar and lots of red wine vinegar, it only tastes better as the days go on. In this version of the Sicilian staple, I borrow nutty creaminess from the Levant in the form of tahini, a rich sesame paste that is a staple in my own kitchen, and many others in the UK these days. I love this with some crusty bread and a green salad, or as a side to some sausages or white fish.

1 Preheat your grill to high. Rub your red peppers with 1 tablespoon of olive oil, then place on a baking tray. Grill for 10 minutes, turning them every so often so they cook evenly. The skins should be blackened, and the peppers basically collapsing.

2 While you grill the peppers, dice your aubergines into 3cm chunks, finely dice your celery and peel and finely dice your red onions.

3 Heat 2 tablespoons of olive oil in a sauté pan over a medium heat. Add half of your aubergines and fry for about 7 minutes until they are golden and totally soft. Remove them from the pan and set aside on a plate, then repeat with the remaining aubergine chunks. Set all your aubergine chunks aside.

4 Add another 3 tablespoons of olive oil to the same pan, then tip in your red onion and celery. Cook for about 15 minutes, still over a medium heat, until super soft.

5 Once your grilled peppers are cool enough to handle, peel off the skins and discard the seeds. Tear the flesh into strips.

6 Return your aubergines to the pan with the onions, and add the red pepper strips too. Pour in your tinned tomatoes, along with the red wine vinegar, sugar, capers and sultanas. Simmer for 15 minutes until the sauce is reduced and the mixture looks thick and jammy.

7 Season to taste with salt and 15 twists of black pepper, then stir through another tablespoon of olive oil. Allow it to cool to room temperature, then serve drizzled with the tahini and sprinkled with toasted sesame seeds.

Charred Hispi Miso Wedge

Serves
4

Cook time
45 minutes

2 hispi cabbages

3 shallots

300g silken tofu

½ tsp Dijon mustard

1½ tbsp brown rice miso paste

1 small garlic clove

juice of ½ lemon

small bunch of chives

25g pickled sushi ginger
(preferably the bright pink stuff)

salt, pepper and rapeseed oil

Wedge salads have a bit of a naff history, but in recent times are being reborn as these incredibly sexy chunks of iceberg lettuce dressed in all kinds of glamorous things. I thought a charred wedge of hispi cabbage deserved a similar makeover, so I've topped it with a creamy sauce made by whizzing up silken tofu with all kinds of lovely things, including miso paste. I sprinkle it with pickled sushi ginger and fried-up crispy shallots, but you could buy shop-bought crispy onions if you're in a hurry. Along with some sushi rice, this would make a very classy dinner.

1 Preheat your oven to 220°C/200°C fan/gas mark 7.

2 Leaving the stalk intact, cut your cabbage in half lengthways, then halve each piece lengthways again so that you have 4 equal-sized wedges. Take a large bowl of water, and submerge your wedges for 5 minutes. The water will get between all the leaves, and the steam this creates will help the cabbage get super tender.

3 Heat a griddle pan over a medium heat. Remove your cabbage wedges from the water and pat them dry on the surface, then rub them all over with 2 tablespoons of rapeseed oil. Place them in the griddle pan, cut-sides down, and sear for 4 minutes on each cut side. You want some really dark griddle lines on there.

4 Remove your cabbage wedges from the pan, and place them cut-sides up on a baking tray. Pop them in the oven for 20 minutes to finish cooking.

5 Meanwhile, make your crispy shallots. Peel your shallots, then cut them into thin rounds.

6 Heat 4 tablespoons of rapeseed oil in a frying pan over a medium heat. While the pan is still cool, add your shallots – this will allow them to crisp up gradually, and stop them from burning. Fry for about 5 minutes until your shallots have just turned golden, then remove them from the pan with a slotted spoon, and leave them to drain on a plate lined with paper towels.

7 To make your dressing, add your silken tofu to a blender, along with your Dijon mustard and miso paste. Peel the garlic clove and add that too, along with the lemon juice. Whizz it all up until you have a thick sauce, and season to taste with salt.

8 Finely chop your chives.

9 Once your cabbage is cooked, arrange the wedges on a serving platter and drizzle over the dressing. Top with the crispy shallots, pickled ginger pieces and chives, and serve.

Mango, Chilli and Halloumi Salad

Serves

4

Cook time

40 minutes

1 red onion

juice of 1 lemon

250g kale

2 ripe mangoes

2 red chillies

2 preserved lemons

3 tbsp apple cider vinegar

450g halloumi

salt and olive oil

The first time I ever ate halloumi was at a wedding in Cyprus when I was seven. I was asleep in a chair at the reception when my mum wafted a piece of halloumi under my nose. I was suddenly awake and having just about as good a time as a person can have. It was crisp and golden on the outside, with a soft and salty middle, and I snaffled up many pieces. To this day, I segue it into as many meals as is acceptable. Halloumi is a natural fit in this salad, though. The saline, squeaky softness is lovely with a sweet and spicy dressing and lil chunks of juicy mango. It feels like a proper summer-y bowl of food that would serve you very well on a scorching day.

1 Peel and finely slice your red onion, then pop this into a bowl. Squeeze over half the lemon juice and sprinkle with ½ teaspoon of salt. Scrunch the onion slices up with your hands to encourage them to start lightly pickling, then set aside until later.

2 Tear the kale leaves from their stalks, throw away the stalks and tear the leaves into bite-sized pieces. Add these to a large mixing bowl with 1 tablespoon of olive oil, the remaining lemon juice and ½ teaspoon of salt, then massage the kale for 5 minutes until it has softened and wilted.

3 Peel your mangoes, then cut the flesh into 2cm chunks. Finely chop one of your chillies, seeds and all.

4 Add 100g of your mango to a blender, along with your chopped chilli, preserved lemons, apple cider vinegar, 9 tablespoons of olive oil and 3 tablespoons of water. Whizz to a smooth consistency, then season to taste with salt.

5 Finely slice the remaining chilli, and cut your halloumi into slices too.

6 Heat 2 tablespoons of olive oil in a frying pan over a medium heat. Add the halloumi slices and fry for 2 minutes on each side until they have developed a nice golden crust.

7 Tip the diced mango, sliced chilli and pickled red onions into your kale bowl. Drizzle over the dressing, and give it all a toss so that everything is coated.

8 Spoon your salad onto plates, and scatter over the halloumi. Serve.

Leek, Fennel and Walnut Gratin

Serves

4

Cook time

1 hour

3 leeks

1 fennel bulb

60g butter

a few thyme sprigs

200ml white wine

20g plain flour

300ml whole milk

140g Cheddar

100ml double cream

40g walnuts

salt and pepper

I like serving a few different veg sides with a roast. I always include something baked and cheesy, and it is often the item my eyes are drawn to most. Even the most ardent fennel-phobe might be converted by this gratin, as the bulb loses its anise-ness when braised this way, and becomes something sweet and mild. Baked with the more traditional leeks and lots of Cheddar, it is deeply comforting.

1   Preheat your oven to 200°C/180°C fan/gas mark 6.

2   Cut your leeks into barrels 4cm tall. Trim your fennel tops (saving any green fronds), then cut the body of the bulb in half. Slice it into wedges through the stalk, so that each slice doesn't fall apart.

3   Melt 20g of the butter in a large frying pan over a medium heat, and pick in your thyme leaves. Add your fennel wedges in a single layer, and let them fry for about 4 minutes until they are starting to caramelise. Flip them over and repeat on the other side.

4   Pour in the wine, and reduce the heat to low. Cut out a square of parchment that fits over the top of the pan, and scrunch it up into a ball. Unscrunch it, then pop it on top of the fennel. Cook for 3 minutes until the wine has almost totally reduced.

5   Remove the parchment from the fennel. Increase the heat to medium-high and cook for another few minutes, until the wine is all gone. Remove the fennel from the pan, and set aside on a plate.

6   Melt another 20g of butter in the same pan, and add your leeks. Fry for about 4 minutes until they are just starting to soften but are still green. It doesn't matter if the leek layers fall apart a bit. Set aside.

7   Melt the remaining 20g of butter in a large saucepan over a medium-low heat. Add flour and cook it out for 2 minutes, then gradually add the milk in small increments, stirring between each addition to make a smooth paste before adding more.

8   Once all the milk has been added, bring it to the boil and let it simmer for 3 minutes. Remove the pan from the heat, then grate in 100g of your Cheddar and stir in the cream. Stir to melt the cheese, then season to taste with salt and 15 twists of black pepper.

9   Arrange your leeks and fennel in a large gratin dish, then pour over the sauce, poking the veg around so that the sauce covers them. Grate over the remaining 40g of Cheddar, then bake for 25 minutes.

10 Meanwhile, scatter your walnuts onto a baking tray. Pop these into the oven for the final 8 minutes, then remove and roughly chop. Serve the gratin topped with the walnuts and the fennel fronds.

Burnt Shallot and Bean Gratin

Serves
6

Cook time
1 hour

4 banana shallots

3 large thyme sprigs

¼ whole nutmeg

150ml double cream

3 × 400g tins of cannellini beans

2 garlic cloves

60g Parmesan or vegetarian hard cheese

salt, pepper and olive oil

When cooking a big winter spread, I personally think that it is a requirement to make something creamy, baked and bubbly. This dish is a favourite among my friends, and it is no wonder. The soft white beans get nestled in a reeeeally *savoury sauce, rich with charred onions, herbs and Parmesan. It is properly beige and, like most beige foods, properly delicious. This would make a phenomenal side for a roast chicken or lamb, but is equally lovely as a meal in and of itself, served with a sharp green salad and a hunk of something bready to mop it up with.*

1 Preheat your grill to high.

2 Halve your shallots lengthways, leaving their skins on.

3 Heat 1 tablespoon of olive oil in a cast-iron skillet or ovenproof frying pan over a high heat. Arrange your shallots in the pan, cut-sides down, and fry for 4 minutes until they have taken on some decent colour.

4 Place your shallot pan under your grill, and cook for 15 minutes until the skins are burnt. Remove from the heat and set aside to cool slightly.

5 Turn off your grill, and preheat your oven to 220°C/200°C fan/ gas mark 7.

6 When they are cool enough to handle, peel the burnt skins off your shallots and discard. Add the shallot flesh to a blender. Pick in your thyme leaves, grate in the nutmeg and pour in your cream, then whizz until you have a smooth, nutty-coloured sauce.

7 Drain your beans in a colander and give them a rinse, then peel and finely chop your garlic.

8 Heat 2 tablespoons of olive oil in a large sauté pan over a medium heat. Add the garlic and fry for a minute until fragrant but not taking on any colour.

9 Tip your beans into the pan, along with 100ml water. Reduce the heat to low and simmer for 5 minutes, breaking down a few of the beans with the back of your spoon to make the mixture a bit creamy. Stir in your burnt onion sauce, and grate in 30g of the Parmesan. Season to taste with salt and 10 grinds of black pepper.

10 Pour your beans into a baking dish, then grate over the remaining Parmesan. Bake in the oven for 30 minutes until golden and bubbly, then serve.

Celeriac and Pancetta Gratin

Serves
8

Cook time
1 hour 15 minutes

2 large celeriacs
(about 750g each)

4 shallots

4 garlic cloves

8 thyme sprigs

200g pancetta

40g butter

600ml double cream

600ml milk

120g Gruyère

30g panko breadcrumbs

½ whole nutmeg

salt and pepper

If Edgar Wright had the Cornetto *trilogy, I have the Cheesy Gratin Trilogy. This is the gripping final instalment! My dad is always tasked with a few specialities in our family (the best fry-up, roast potatoes, cassoulet), but the pièce de résistance is his dauphinoise potatoes, rich with nutmeg and black pepper, baked in enormous trays for the masses. I absolutely had to have a root veg gratin of sorts in this book to honour this tradition, and I landed on this earthy number as the lucky winner. Celeriac gives sweetness and nuttiness, making it one of the dreamiest roast dinner accompaniments you could imagine. It is as comforting as the crackliest fireplace, the biggest hug, the softest blanket. Serve with some crusty bread, a roast chicken or a crisp green salad.*

1 Preheat the oven to 190°C/170°C fan/gas mark 5½.

2 Start by prepping your vegetables. Peel your celeriacs and cut them in half, then chop the halves into thin slices. Peel, halve and slice your shallots. Grate your garlic and pick your thyme leaves from their tough stalks.

3 Set a large saucepan over a low heat. Add the pancetta and let it gently cook for 5 minutes, or until it has rendered out its fat and crisped up nicely. Remove it from the pan with a slotted spoon and set aside on a plate.

4 Melt your butter in the same saucepan over a low-medium heat. Add the shallots and cook for 10 minutes until they are totally soft and sweet. Add the garlic and thyme leaves and cook for another minute, then pour in the cream and milk. Season with salt to taste, and grind in about 30 twists of black pepper. You want it to be just a little bit less salty than if you were going to eat it at this point. Add your celeriac and simmer gently for 15 minutes, until your sauce has thickened and the celeriac is just tender.

5 Meanwhile, grate the Gruyère into a bowl. Add the panko breadcrumbs and mix to combine, then set this aside until later.

6 When your celeriac is tender, add a generous grating of nutmeg, then add the crispy pancetta to the pan and gently fold it through to combine.

7 Pour your celeriac mixture into a 32 × 25cm baking dish. Cover the dish with foil and bake for 20 minutes.

8 After 20 minutes, remove the foil, then sprinkle on the breadcrumbs and cheese. Bake for another 15 minutes until golden and bubbly.

9 Serve it up.

Braised Greens and Radishes

Serves
6 as a side

Cook time
45 minutes

400g greens (spring greens, kale, cavolo nero or Swiss chard would be excellent here)

240g radishes

2 garlic cloves

½ tsp chilli flakes

1 tsp fennel seeds

juice of ½ lemon

salt and olive oil

The virtuous reputation of greens may make them seem like a boring side dish to some, but I find I come back to them time and time again. There is nothing in the vegetable world simpler and more nourishing to me. A crunchy, raw radish is such a good thing that for years, I resisted cooking them. How gutted I was when I realised that a cooked radish is equally delightful, and I had wasted years shunning them! Fear not: I have made up for lost time. I love the way that the vibrant pink outsides bleed into the white middles, giving you blushed little things that brighten up any side dish. My favourite way to eat them is braised alongside garlicky greens – a phenomenal spring side. This would also be really good with a dollop of ricotta and some crusty toast for something more substantial.

1 Remove and discard the stalks from your greens, then tear the leaves in half to give you large pieces. Remove and discard the green stalks from your radishes, then halve them. Peel and finely slice your garlic cloves.

2 Heat 4 tablespoons of olive oil in a large pan with a lid over a medium-low heat. Add your garlic, chilli flakes and fennel seeds, and cook gently for 1 minute until the garlic just starts to turn golden on the edges. Add your greens and radishes to the pan, then sprinkle in 1 teaspoon of salt and pour in 150ml water. Cover with a lid, then reduce the heat to as low as it will go, and cook very gently for 20 minutes.

3 When you're ready to serve, season your veg with the lemon juice, then enjoy.

Teriyaki Squash with Ginger-Whipped Tofu

Serves
4

Cook time
1 hour

280g firm tofu

1 large butternut squash

4cm knob of ginger

1 garlic clove

50g caster sugar

80ml light soy sauce

2 tbsp cornflour

1 tsp rice wine vinegar

1 tbsp sesame oil

4 spring onions

1 tbsp shichimi togarashi

salt and vegetable oil

Whipped tofu is a lovely way to eat a food that some people struggle with. It has the thick silkiness of hummus, with the sweetness of tofu. I first ate it at a Mam Sham party, where we were fed by Supaya Ramen, and have been making it ever since. Butternut squash is the queen of autumn in my books, and I love it drizzled with this teriyaki-esque sauce. It deserves to be eaten in a cosy room with frosted windows, while leaves crunch outside.

1 Preheat your oven to 210°C/190°C fan/gas mark 6½ and line a large baking tray with baking parchment.

2 Place your tofu on a plate lined with paper towels. Put another paper towel on top, then place a heavy pan on this, to press the tofu and squeeze out excess liquid. Leave your tofu to press.

3 Peel your butternut squash, then halve it vertically. Scoop out the seeds. Halve vertically again, so you have 4 equal-sized wedges. Lay them on the prepared baking tray, drizzle with 1 tablespoon of vegetable oil and a teaspoon of salt, and rub it all in. Roast for 45–50 minutes, until the squash is tender and with charred edges.

4 Meanwhile, make your teriyaki sauce. Thinly slice the ginger and bash the garlic clove, then chop it in half. Pop half the ginger and half the garlic into a saucepan over a medium-low heat, with the caster sugar, soy sauce and 225ml water. Bring to a gentle simmer for about for 5 minutes, stirring until the sugar has dissolved.

5 In a small bowl, mix the cornflour with 2 tablespoons of water to form a paste. Pour this into your sauce, and whisk it in to dissolve. Bring to the boil, then simmer for 5 minutes. It should be drizzle-able and glossy. Stir in your rice wine vinegar, then set aside.

6 To make the whipped tofu, tip your pressed tofu into a blender, along with the sesame oil, 100ml water, and the remaining ginger and garlic. Whizz it to a smooth paste – it should be a little thinner than supermarket hummus – then season to taste with salt.

7 Finely slice your spring onions, green parts and all. Heat 6 tablespoons of vegetable oil in a medium-sized frying pan over a medium heat. Tip in your spring onions and fry them for about 3 minutes, or until they start to look a bit frazzled and are just start turning golden on the edges. Remove them from the pan with a slotted spoon, and set aside on a plate lined with paper towels.

8 Remove the ginger and garlic chunks from the sauce, then gently warm it through. To serve, swoosh your whipped tofu onto a serving platter, top with the squash and drizzle over the teriyaki sauce. Sprinkle over your spring onions and togarashi, then enjoy.

Sweet Stuff

We humans love categorising things to help us understand the world better. I have always put myself firmly in the camp of Savoury Gal and not in camp Dessert Person, but, as with most things, the situation is more nuanced. The truth is, I love the food that comes before pudding so much that I often do not have capacity for another mouthful, so I don't tend to order desserts in restaurants. Also, as a cook who is pretty loosey-goosey with measurements, cooking sweeter things can be stressful, as cakes and custards require more precision. This chapter is filled with puddings you can make with little skill or inclination, that can all be prepared ahead of time without you having to sweat. I won't judge you if you can't be bothered, though. There's nothing wrong with whipping out some ice lollies, berries or chocolate at the end of a meal.

Sticky Banana Cake

Serves
8

Cook time
1 hour, plus cooling

140g butter, *plus extra
for greasing*

175g soft light brown sugar

3 cardamom pods

1 star anise

1 cinnamon stick

**3 medium unripe bananas,
or 2 large ones**

1 egg

3 ripe bananas

50g natural yoghurt

1 tsp vanilla extract

225g plain flour

½ tsp ground cinnamon

½ tsp ground cardamom

1 tsp bicarbonate of soda

150ml double cream, *to serve*

½ tsp salt

My mum is many wonderful things, but is known to my friends as a killer banana bread-maker. Whenever I went back up to uni, she would pack me off with a soft banana loaf swirled with melted toffees, and it would get demolished at great speed. I am not much of a cake lover, but I'm not sure how a person couldn't love banana bread. It is one of the great childhood-nostalgia foods to me, up there with bangers, mash and baked beans as a food that makes me feel fantastic. If you have a friend who also deserves to feel fantastic, then you should make them this cake. I've reinvented it somewhat for this version, and loaded it up with a spiced caramel. You get the stickiness of an upside-down cake, balanced by the almost savouriness of the banana bread.

1 Preheat your oven to 180°C/160°C fan/gas mark 4. Grease a 20cm cake tin with butter and line with baking parchment, covering the base and the sides.

2 Combine 40g of the butter and 75g of the sugar in a saucepan, along with your cardamom pods, star anise and cinnamon stick. Cook it over a medium heat until your sugar has dissolved, and it has all melded into a sticky caramel sauce. Let the spices infuse in the pan for 5 minutes, then pour the mixture into the base of your cake tin and spread it out.

3 Cut your unripe bananas into rounds, and arrange these on the base of the cake tin.

4 Add your remaining butter and sugar to a large mixing bowl, and whisk together with electric beaters until pale and fluffy. Crack in the egg, and whisk again until combined.

5 Peel your ripe bananas and mash these up in a separate bowl with a fork. Add the mashed flesh to the mixing bowl, along with your yoghurt and vanilla extract. Whisk the mixture until combined, then sift in your flour, ground cinnamon, ground cardamom, bicarbonate of soda and salt, and whisk again until just combined.

6 Pour your cake batter into the tin, then bake in the centre of your oven for 45 minutes. Insert a skewer to check if it is done – it should come out clean when it's ready.

7 Let your cake cool in its tin for 30 minutes, then place a plate on top of the tin and flip it over to turn out the cake. Allow it to cool for about 20 minutes if you want to eat it warm, or longer if you want to eat it cold. Carefully peel off the parchment, carve it into pieces and serve with double cream poured over. It will keep for 3 days in an airtight tin.

Chocolate and Cherry Meringue Tower

Serves
8–10

Cook time
1 hour 30 minutes, plus cooling

40g dark chocolate,
plus 15g for grating on top

4 large egg whites (*save the yolks
for another occasion*)

230g caster sugar

450g frozen cherries

2 tbsp kirsch (*optional*)

300ml double cream

25g icing sugar

Jeremy Lee is the executive chef at Quo Vadis in Soho, the first and only proper restaurant I ever worked in, and he is famous for making the most fabulous puddings in London, if not the world. Working there, I assembled many enormous meringue towers, rich with cream, fruit and toasted nuts. This pud is inspired by my time there. It features Black Forest flavours; my dad is passionate about chocolate, cherries and cream as a combination, so when making him a pud, I often use these flavours. This one's for you, Dad! This is a proper show-stopping dessert – expect oohs and aahs as you wheel it out of the kitchen.

1 Preheat your oven to 140°C/120°C fan/gas mark 1 and line 2 large baking trays with baking parchment.

2 Break the chocolate into a heatproof bowl, and microwave it in bursts until it is melted. Alternatively, pop the chocolate into a heatproof bowl set over a simmering pan of water, and let it gently melt. Allow it to cool slightly.

3 Tip your egg whites into a large mixing bowl, and weigh out 200g of your sugar in a separate bowl. Using electric beaters, whisk the egg whites to stiff peaks. Add a couple of heaped spoonfuls of the sugar, then whisk again until you get stiff peaks. Continue adding the sugar like this until all 200g has been incorporated, and you have a thick, glossy mixture in the bowl.

4 Pour your melted chocolate into the bowl, and gently fold it through as streaks. Take generous spoonfuls of this meringue mixture, and dollop them onto the prepared baking trays in glossy heaps, spaced well apart. You should get about 10 meringues. Place both trays in the oven, and bake them for 1 hour.

5 Meanwhile, add your cherries to a saucepan over a medium heat, along with your remaining 30g of sugar. Bring the mixture to the boil, then reduce the heat to low and simmer gently for 20 minutes, or until the liquid has a thin, syrupy consistency. Stir in the kirsch, if using, then leave it to cool.

6 Pour your double cream into a medium mixing bowl, and add the icing sugar. Whisk with electric beaters until it thickens into soft peaks. Be careful not to overdo it – you don't want it to look fluffy.

7 Allow your meringues to cool completely. When ready to serve, spoon a little cream onto your chosen serving plate. Add a few meringues on top, and dollop over some cream and cherry compote. Continue to stack meringues, cream and compote on top until they are all used up. Grate over a little more chocolate, then serve.

Chocolate Coconut Cream Pie

Serves
10

Cook time
1 hour, plus chilling

For the base
30g coconut flakes

250g digestive biscuits
*(gluten-free if necessary,
and check the ingredients
if you're vegan)*

100g vegan butter,
plus extra for greasing

For the filling
**2 x 400g tins of full-fat
coconut milk,** *chilled*

1 tbsp coconut oil

280g dark chocolate

For the topping
20g coconut flakes

2 tbsp maple syrup

**2 x 400g tins of full-fat
coconut milk,** *chilled*

5 tbsp icing sugar

½ tsp vanilla extract

20g dark chocolate

flaky sea salt

Tip

*Buy tins of coconut milk
with the highest percentage of
coconut possible. Do not shake
before using or you won't get
the thick cream on top.*

I am thrilled to have reached an age where I recognise that a Bounty is the best one in the Celebrations box. I decided to lean in to the chocolate-and-coconut alliance with this plant-based pud to make a Bounty-esque, full-on coconutty dessert. Spare liquid from the coconut milk tins is great in smoothies.

1 First, prepare the base. Toast the coconut flakes in a dry frying pan over a medium heat for 5 minutes until they are lightly golden.

2 Tip your toasted coconut flakes into a food processor, along with your digestive biscuits, and pulse them to very fine crumbs. Melt your vegan butter, then stir this through.

3 Grease a 20cm loose-bottomed tart tin with butter and line the base with a round of baking parchment. Add your biscuit-crumb mixture and push it into the base and up the sides so that the tin is evenly lined, using the base of a glass to level the bottom and your fingers to level the sides. Pop into the fridge for an hour so it can firm up.

4 To make the filling, open the chilled tins of coconut milk, and scoop out all of the solid white layer on top. Place in a heatproof bowl, along with the coconut oil, and heat in the microwave in 30-second bursts, stirring in between each one, until it is steaming but not bubbling (alternatively, you can do this in a saucepan on the hob).

5 Finely chop your chocolate, then pop it into a large mixing bowl. Pour your hot coconut milk over the chocolate and let it stand for 2 minutes, then give it a mix to make sure the chocolate melts.

6 Remove your tart case from the fridge, then pour the chocolate mixture into it. Return it to the fridge to chill for 2 hours.

7 Preheat your oven to 180°C/160°C fan/gas mark 4 and line a medium-sized baking tray with baking parchment.

8 To prepare the topping, tip the coconut flakes into the prepared baking tray and add your maple syrup, plus ½ teaspoon of flaky sea salt. Gently mix it together so that the syrup coats all the coconut flakes, but make sure you don't break up the flakes too much. Bake for 10 minutes, then leave them to cool completely and firm up.

9 Open your chilled tins of coconut milk, and scoop out 250g of the solid layer at the top. Add this to a mixing bowl, along with your icing sugar and vanilla extract, and whisk until thick and smooth.

10 When your filling is set, spoon your coconut cream over the top. Grate over the dark chocolate, and sprinkle over your coconut flakes. Remove the tart from the tin, then serve.

Apricot and Ricotta Cake

Serves

8

Cook time

1 hour 30 minutes, plus cooling

120g softened butter,
plus extra for greasing

250g ricotta

200g ground almonds

1 tsp baking powder

3 eggs

200g caster sugar

zest of 1 lemon

1 tsp vanilla extract

5 apricots

1 tbsp demerara sugar

2 tbsp flaked almonds

icing sugar, *to serve*

salt

Tip

This cake freezes beautifully once it is cooked – just make sure it is wrapped tightly in cling film.

The particularity of making cakes can be a stressful thing. As I have said, I am not a precise cook, and too much technique can put me off cooking a recipe. This recipe is designed to not be difficult at all, and results in a cake with an intentionally moist crumb, so you don't have to worry about making it too light. I prefer cakes with a soft crumb, and that's what we have here, thanks to the ricotta whipped into the batter, and the jammy fruit baked into it. It is incidentally gluten-free too, for the coeliac queens out there, though gluten-lovers will notice no difference.

1 Preheat your oven to 200°C/180°C fan/gas mark 6.

2 Grease a 20cm springform cake tin with butter and line with baking parchment – you want the parchment to cover the base and sides of the tin. I do this by cutting out a large circle, then scrunching it up and pushing it into the sides and base.

3 Pop your ricotta into a sieve set over a bowl, and set aside to let any excess water drain off.

4 Mix your ground almonds, baking powder and ½ teaspoon of salt in a medium-sized bowl. Set these aside until later.

5 Separate your eggs into yolks and whites, adding your yolks to a small bowl and your whites to a separate medium-sized one. With electric beaters, whisk your egg whites to soft peaks. Set aside.

6 Combine your sugar and butter in a large mixing bowl and whisk together with electric beaters until they are thick, pale and fluffy. Add your egg yolks and beat these in, too.

7 Grate in your lemon zest, then add the vanilla extract and ricotta. Whisk to combine.

8 Sift in your dry ingredients, then fold gently to combine without knocking out the air. Spoon in your egg whites, again gently folding them in to combine without knocking out too much air.

9 Halve your apricots and remove the stones.

10 Pour your batter into the tin, then arrange your apricot halves on top. Sprinkle the cake with demerara sugar and flaked almonds.

11 Bake in the centre of the oven for 30 minutes. When this time is up, cover the surface of the cake with parchment, and cook for another 30 minutes, or until a skewer inserted into the centre comes out clean.

12 Once the cake has cooled, remove it from its tin, dust the top with icing sugar, then slice it into wedges and serve.

Rhubarb and Custard Croissant Pudding

Serves
6–8

Cook time
1 hour, plus resting

400g forced rhubarb

120g caster sugar

zest of 1 orange and juice of ½

butter, for greasing

300ml double cream

300ml whole milk

4 eggs

1 tsp vanilla bean paste

8 croissants

2 tbsp icing sugar,
for dusting

150ml single cream,
to serve

Rhubarb and custard is one of the most classic British dessert combinations, and it isn't hard to see why. Tangy, tart rhubarb on its own can be pretty intense, but it's softened when paired with creamy, egg-enriched custard. While making custard itself can be tricky – and can result in a pan of sweet scrambled eggs – making a bread pudding gives you custardy vibes without any of the risk. This is a real bang-it-together dessert that would be an absolute dream to serve up after a springtime Sunday lunch, when blushing pink forced rhubarb is in its prime. You'll have lots of rhubarb syrup left over – this makes a phenomenal cocktail ingredient.

1 Preheat your oven to 200°C/180°C fan/gas mark 6.

2 Cut your rhubarb into 5cm lengths. Add these to a large baking tray, then sprinkle over 50g of your caster sugar and half the orange zest. Squeeze over the orange juice, then give everything a really good toss so that all the rhubarb is coated in the sugar and juice. Rearrange the rhubarb into a single layer. Cover the tray with foil, then roast for 15 minutes. Remove from the oven and leave it to cool a bit.

3 Reduce the oven temperature to 180°C/160°C fan/gas mark 4 and grease a roughly 32 × 25cm baking dish with butter.

4 Pour the cream and milk into a small saucepan over a medium heat, and bring it up to a simmer. Remove from the heat. Crack your eggs into a bowl, then pour in the remaining caster sugar. Whisk until the eggs and sugar are totally combined. Switch your whisk for a spatula at this point to avoid beating too much air into your custard. Gradually pour in your warm cream mixture, beating all the while with your spatula until the mixture is totally combined. Add the vanilla bean paste, and briefly mix again.

5 Cut your croissants in half through the middle. Arrange half of them in the prepared baking dish, cut-side up, then spoon in about half of your roasted rhubarb with a slotted spoon, making sure not to add too much syrup. Arrange your remaining croissants on top with the ridged 'presentation side' up. Top with about half of the remaining rhubarb, then pour your custard mixture over the top. Let your pudding sit for 30 minutes so that the croissants absorb the custard, then bake for 20 minutes, or until it is gently set.

6 Spoon over your remaining rhubarb and a little of its syrup, then dust with icing sugar. Serve warm, with a drizzle of single cream.

Hazelnut Tiramisu

Serves

6

Prep time
30 minutes, plus setting

280ml freshly brewed coffee

50ml marsala wine

4 eggs

90g caster sugar

500g mascarpone

150g hazelnut butter

175g sponge fingers

2 tbsp cocoa powder

A Kinder Bueno is one of those chocolate bars that I have to try to not make eye contact with when I pass them in the shops. I cannot resist them. That hazelnut cream! How could you not want to eat that? I wanted to create a pud that took on that heavenly nutty, creamy quality, and could not think of a better dessert to do it with than a tiramisu. I know you shouldn't choose a favourite child, but this is probably my favourite pud in the book. It is quick and easy to assemble ahead of time too, so minimal stress and effort.

1 Pour your coffee into a bowl and add your marsala. Allow the mixture to cool.

2 Separate your egg whites and yolks into two separate mixing bowls. Add half of your sugar to the egg whites, then whisk them to soft peaks using electric beaters.

3 Pour the rest of your sugar into the egg yolks, then whisk with your electric beaters until they are pale and mousse-like. Tip in your mascarpone and hazelnut butter, then whisk again briefly until combined.

4 Add about a quarter of your egg whites to the mascarpone bowl, and beat until combined. Now add half of your remaining egg whites, and gently fold these into the mixture with a large metal spoon. Repeat with the remaining egg whites.

5 Dip half of your sponge fingers into the coffee mixture for a couple of seconds to flavour them, but not for so long that they fall apart. Arrange these sponge fingers side by side in the base of a 32 x 25cm baking dish.

6 Spread over half of your mascarpone mixture, then dip your remaining sponge fingers in the coffee mixture, and arrange these on top. Spread over your remaining mascarpone mixture, then put your tiramisu in the fridge to set, ideally overnight, but for at least a few hours.

7 When you are ready to serve, dust the surface of your tiramisu with sifted cocoa powder, then cut it into chunky pieces and serve.

Tip

Hazelnut butter can easily be found online, or in health food shops, and is very much worth seeking out.

Salted Chocolate Brûlée Pots

Serves
6

Cook time
1 hour, plus setting

600ml double cream

1 tsp vanilla bean paste

100g dark chocolate

6 large egg yolks

50g caster sugar, *plus 6 tbsp for sprinkling*

flaky salt

There aren't many puddings sexier than a crème brûlée. It was a 90s dinner-party classic with good reason. The luxuriousness of silky set custard with a satisfying sugar snap on top is unrivalled. It's had an uncomplicated makeover here with the addition of some dark chocolate and flaky sea salt, to give it a distinctly 2020s edge. I'm rather out of practice when it comes to wooing people, but I imagine that the hottie you are cooking for on your third date would be really quite besotted with you if you gave them this for afters. Equally, the friends you love the best in the world will probably want to give you a very big hug if you gave them this to round off a cosy dinner. I recommend getting a blowtorch if you are going to brûlée – I find grills have a habit of ruining your work, turning what was once luscious and velvety into scrambled eggs.

1 Preheat your oven to 170°C/150°C fan/gas mark 3½.

2 Pour your double cream into a saucepan, along with your vanilla bean paste. Bring it to a very gentle simmer.

3 Very finely chop your chocolate, then add it to a heatproof measuring jug. Once your cream is steaming, but not too hot, pour it over your chocolate. Let it stand for 2 minutes before mixing it with a spatula to melt the chocolate into the cream.

4 In a bowl, beat your egg yolks with the sugar until they are just combined. Pour the chocolatey cream over this egg mixture, beating it steadily with your spatula as you pour to mix it all together. Add a heaped teaspoon of flaky sea salt, and mix again.

5 Take six 7cm ramekins and arrange them in a deep roasting tin. Pour your custard mixture into your ramekins through a small sieve (this will get rid of any eggy bits). Carefully pour water into the roasting tin so that it sits about a third of the way up the sides of your ramekins. Cover the top of the roasting tray tightly with foil, then carefully place your tray into the oven, making sure the water doesn't splash into the custard. Bake for 30 minutes; when they are done, they should wobble when lightly shaken, with a firmer set around the edges and a liquid-y middle. They will set further as they cool, so don't be alarmed if they feel quite wet still.

6 Carefully remove the pots from their water bath, and leave them to cool to room temperature. Once they are cool, pop them into the fridge to chill overnight, or for at least 4 hours.

7 When you are ready to serve, remove the pots from the fridge. Sprinkle with the remaining sugar and blowtorch them. Serve.

Lemon Meringue Ice Cream Cake

Serves

10

Cook time

25 minutes, plus chilling

1 litre thick vanilla ice cream

(I use Mackie's)

80g butter

200g shortbread biscuits

5 shop-bought meringue nests

400g lemon curd

One of the reasons why I am often reluctant to make a pudding is the time and oven space it can occupy. This one is ideal because it goes against all odds and takes up neither of those things. It entails buying a handful of shop-bought ingredients, casually layering them, then freezing to create a zingy, creamy masterpiece. It's got all the flavours of a lemon meringue pie, but with far less faff. I can see it going down an absolute treat in the height of summer, as the barbecue coals cool down and the twelfth jug of Pimm's is assembled.

1 Remove your ice cream from the freezer and leave it to stand for 15 minutes so it softens slightly.

2 Pop your butter into a small saucepan, and warm it over a gentle heat until it is just melted. Alternatively, do this in a microwave.

3 Place your shortbread biscuits in a food processor, and whizz to form fine crumbs. Pour the crumbs into your melted butter, and mix together to combine.

4 Crush your meringue nests into pieces with your hands.

5 Line a 20cm springform cake tin with a couple of layers of cling film. Pour in your shortbread crumbs mixture, and press this into the tin in an even layer. Spoon a little of your lemon curd down the edges of your tin. Spoon some of your ice cream into the base, then swirl through 4 tablespoons of the lemon curd. Scatter over a handful of meringue, then keep layering like this until all your mixtures are used up, finishing with a couple of blobs of lemon curd and a handful of meringue. Cover the top tightly with more cling film and freeze for at least 4 hours, or until totally set.

6 When you are ready to serve, get your 'cake' out of the freezer. Pop it out of the case and unwrap the cling film, then carefully place it on a plate. Cut into slices to serve.

Tip

This would keep for about a month in the freezer, so why not make it in advance and save it for pudding emergencies?

Pineapple Mar-granita

Serves
4

Cook time
25 minutes, plus freezing

zest and juice of 5 limes

150g caster sugar

1 small pineapple

150ml tequila

25ml triple sec

Is it a pudding? Is it a cocktail? Who's to say? I personally think that a cocktail can be a pudding – that sweet little finisher to mark the end of the feast, and the beginning of the rest of your night. It is the turning point that indicates that things are about to get a little wild. Tequila is the substance with the most potential to take an evening in a new and raucous direction. My friends have developed a fixation with a drink called a Craig David, where you take a shot of pineapple juice, then a shot of tequila, then a shot of pineapple again. The craze has extended into my family, where many evenings are now punctuated with rounds of this sweet, acidic shot. This granita takes those flavours and mixes them into the most refreshing little thing. On a balmy summer evening, this would be a very classy way to cleanse your palate of the savoury stuff, before moving on to a little dance party.

1 Zest your limes into a small saucepan, then pour in the sugar and 150ml water. Gently bring it to a simmer over a medium-low heat, stirring occasionally to encourage the sugar to dissolve. Once dissolved, remove the pan from the heat and allow the syrup to cool to room temperature.

2 Cut the skin off your pineapple, then cut the flesh into chunks. Weigh out 300g of it to use in this recipe – you can snack on the rest as you go.

3 Once your syrup has cooled, pour it into a blender. Add your pineapple chunks and whizz together until you have a smooth liquid. Skim any foam off the top.

4 Add your lime juice, along with the tequila and triple sec. Give it a stir so that all the ingredients are combined.

5 Pour the mixture into a shallow Tupperware container, then pop on the lid and place it into the freezer for an hour.

6 Remove from the freezer, and scrape it up with a fork. Return it to the freezer, and repeat this step every hour for 4 hours, until you have a grainy ice-crystal texture. It will be sludgy at first, but will become increasingly crystalised as time goes on.

7 Spoon the granita into glasses, and serve it up.

Tip
You can prepare this granita up to 2 months in advance and keep it in the freezer.

How not to lose your mind when hosting

If you are having people round for a meal, whether it's two people or 20, there are a few things you can do to make it a more enjoyable experience. Take it from a person who has hosted a few dinners in her time, and in the early days burst into tears at most of them because she'd bitten off more than she could chew. No tears for you, dear reader! Here are my top tips.

1.

Everyone will feel more relaxed, yourself included, if you give people a bowl of crisps. If your timings are off and the food is an hour late, you can be at peace with the knowledge that your guests aren't starving. Crisps are actually obligatory in my mind.

2.

Nobody minds if you don't have ten matching plates, glasses and napkins. If anything, an eclectic mixture of chipped Ikea plates, your great aunt's cabbage bowl and some old floral china from a charity shop make for a more interesting and aesthetically pleasing spread.

3.

Light candles. Lots of them. Chunky pillars, tealights and long ones twisted into old bottles make any table look more atmospheric and glam.

4.

You don't need to make everything yourself. In fact, it is better if you don't attempt to. You'll have less washing-up if you don't make your own hummus; anyway, the good people of Sainsbury's have already perfected it. Ditto on crisps, breads and puddings. Zhuzh things up in your own bowls and plates – with a little dressing-up, it will look homemade anyway.

5.

The washing-up can wait until the morning.

6.

Choose which plates to serve things on ahead of time. You can even be extra like me and pop a sticky note on them to remind yourself about which dish goes where.

7.

An overcrowded oven takes much longer time to cook things. Never forget this. I once had a disaster where a dauphinoise took 2½ hours to cook. Never again.

8.

People are generally thrilled to eat anything that they didn't have to cook themselves. Never apologise for the cooking when you sit down to eat – your guests will be loving it, no matter what you serve up.

9.

If someone is coming round to eat after work, prep something to eat the day before. Future-you will be so grateful to past-you.

10.

Making a fresh pudding isn't that important in my mind. A cold bar of chocolate from the fridge served alongside a bit of cheese normally scratches the itch just fine.

Dinner plans

On the occasion that you are having a few people round for slap-up dinner, and you don't know what might go with what, here are some examples of dishes that I think would be really quite lovely together.

Garden Do

Farinata with Datterini and Pine Nut Salsa
(page 15)
Green Harissa Spinach Pie (page 130)
Spiced Tomatoey Chickpeas with Tzatziki (page 78)
Anchovy and Parmesan Courgette Salad (page 199)
Sleepy Flatbreads (page 177)
Hazelnut Tiramisu (page 236)

Spicy Vibes

Corn Pakoras (page 26)
Sticky Lamb Meatball Chaat (page 139)
Paneer Skewers with Bombay Slaw (pages 142–143)
Curried Potato Salad (page 168)
Sticky Tamarind Carrots with Green Chilli Yoghurt
(page 184)
Chocolate Coconut Cream Pie (page 230)

Midweek Ease

Puttanesca Gildas (page 21)
Pulled Oyster Mushroom Ragu (page 102)
Bitter Leaves with Butter Bean Croutons (page 202)
Honestly, just get a couple of bars of chocolate
out the fridge!

Salad Freak

Bloody Mary Prawn Cocktail Cups (page 30)

Endive Cups with Goat's Cheese and Pickled Walnuts
(page 24)

Candied Chilli and Pistachio Whipped Ricotta
(page 20)

Crispy Tofu, Grapefruit and Peanut Salad (page 191)

All the Greens, Apple and Ginger Salad (page 197)

Beetroot, Burrata and Curry Leaf Salad (page 200)

Pineapple Mar-granita (page 243)

Cosy Evening

Mushroom Parfait Toasts (page 33)

Green Olive Baked Camembert (page 22)

Spiced Meatballs with Dates and Chickpeas
(page 126)

Cheesy Spring Onion and Potato Pie (page 171)

Ale-Braised Oyster Mushrooms (page 154)

Braised Greens and Radishes (page 221)

Rhubarb and Custard Croissant Pudding (page 235)

Alt Roast

Smoked Trout and Pickle Pumpernickel Toasts
(page 29)

Life-Saving Garlic Chicken (page 146)

Squash, Cheddar and Chilli Cake (page 137)

Leek, Fennel and Walnut Gratin (page 216)

Potatoes for Mum (page 181)

Chocolate and Cherry Meringue Tower (page 228)

Index

A

ale-braised oyster mushrooms 154
all the greens, apple and ginger
  salad 197
all the greens fried rice with crispy
  sesame egg 62–3
all-the-fishes stew with piri-piri oil
  155–7
almonds
  apricot and ricotta cake 232–3
  charred cauliflower with
    prosciutto and almonds 186–7
anchovies
  anchovy and Parmesan
    courgette salad 198–9
  puttanesca gildas 21
  squash, anchovy and
    mascarpone pasta 90–1
apples
  all the greens, apple and ginger
    salad 197
apricot and ricotta cake 232–3
artichoke hearts 14
  crispy artichoke hearts with feta
    and olive dip 40–1
aubergines
  burnt aubergine curry with
    chickpea pancakes 48–9
  lamb and charred pepper beans
    71
  sesame caponata 210–11

B

banana cake, sticky 226–7
beans
  all the greens fried rice with
    crispy sesame egg 62–3
  all the pickles potato salad
    170
  bitter leaves with butter bean
    croutons 202–3
  burnt lime and honey chicken
    kebabs 123–5
  burnt shallot and bean gratin
    218–19
  celeriac schnitzel with charred
    pepper salsa 152–3
  coconut chicken and bean salad
    with jammy shallots 68–70
  creamy sausage, leek and bean
    stew 52–3
  lamb and charred pepper beans
    71

sizzly leek vinaigrette with
  green yoghurt beans 208–9
tofu traybake tacos 54–5
beef
  coconut and chilli beef shin pie
    134–5
  spiced meatballs with dates and
    chickpeas 126–7
beetroot, burrata and curry leaf
  salad 200–1
Bloody Mary prawn cocktail cups
  30
Bombay mix
  Bombay mix chicken with
    tamarind broccoli 76–7
  Bombay slaw 142, 143
bread
  cheesy garlic flatbreads 178–9
  miso onion gnocchi 114–15
  mushroom parfait toasts 33–4
  sleepy flatbreads 177
broccoli
  all the greens, apple and ginger
    salad 197
  all the greens fried rice with
    crispy sesame egg 62–3
  Bombay mix chicken with
    tamarind broccoli 76–7
  charred broccoli and curried
    lentil salad 194–6
Brussels sprouts
  double sprout, blue cheese and
    cranberry salad 192–3
butter 9
  chicken butter, pancetta and
    leek tagliatelle 88–9
butternut squash
  sausage, squash and taleggio
    cheese traybake 66–7
  squash, anchovy and
    mascarpone pasta 90–1
  squash, Cheddar and chilli cake
    136–8
  teriyaki squash with ginger-
    whipped tofu 222–3

C

cabbage
  all the greens, apple and ginger
    salad 197
  cauliflower shawarma bowls 44–5
  charred hispi miso wedge
    212–13

spiced lamb shoulder with
  Bombay slaw 143–5
Camembert, olive baked 22–3
carrots 14
  carrot pickle 160
  sticky tamarind carrots with
    green chilli yoghurt 184–5
cauliflower
  brown butter cauliflower risotto
    174–6
  cauliflower shawarma bowls
    44–5
  charred cauliflower with
    prosciutto and almonds 186–7
cavolo and taleggio pasta 84–5
celeriac
  celeriac and pancetta gratin 220
  celeriac schnitzel with charred
    pepper salsa 152–3
chaat masala 139
cheese
  (almost) no-cook tomato and
    ricotta pasta 98–9
  anchovy and Parmesan
    courgette salad 198–9
  baked feta with honey harissa
    aubergines 206–7
  beetroot, burrata and curry leaf
    salad 200–1
  brown butter cauliflower risotto
    174–6
  burnt shallot and bean gratin
    218–19
  candied chilli and pistachio
    whipped ricotta 20
  cavolo and taleggio pasta 84–5
  celeriac and pancetta gratin 220
  cheat's sausage and walnut
    lasagne 82–3
  cheeseboard Arancini 31–2
  cheesy garlic flatbreads 178–9
  cheesy spring onion and potato
    pie 171–3
  chestnut and mushroom rotolo
    92–4
  chicken and ricotta meatballs
    with green spaghetti 96–7
  chipotle vodka gnocchi bake
    110–11
  crispy artichoke hearts with feta
    and olive dip 40–1
  curried chicken legs with cheesy
    polenta 128–9

Acknowledgements

Apologies if this reads a bit like an Oscars acceptance speech, but I am so filled with gratitude for an extraordinary amount of people. So, here we go.

The biggest thanks goes to every single one of you who has bought this book, and shown me love on my journey so far. The novelty of you enjoying my food will never wear off. The community I have found online, and the confidence it has given me, is what brought this book to life. This is for each and every one of you! You are top babes.

To Emily Brickell, Lizzy Gray and the whole Ebury squad. You have been a fountain of kindness and wisdom since day dot. Thank you for helping me to shape lots of garbled thoughts into a piece of work that (hopefully) makes sense.

Shooting the photography for this book was one of the most precious experiences of my life, and the most mega group effort. I could not have felt more held by this team! Thank you to Lizzie Mayson for your phenomenal photography, and Esther Clark for the best damn food styling I ever could have hoped for. You totally got my vision, and brought it to life in the most stunning way. Both of you have an incredible knack for creating scenes that look real and messy and natural, and I am so grateful to you both for safely delivering the most beautiful baby I could have wished for into the world. Thank you also to Caitlin, El, Abbie, Ollie, Romy and Tamia for your assistance across the shoots.

Props are *very* important to me, and Hannah Wilkinson absolutely smashed the brief, sourcing so many gorg vintage plates that could not have felt more 'me'. I also wanted to shout out Tash Hart (@clayandlimes) for creating some incredible bespoke ceramics for the book. Thanks both!

Thanks to the power house that is Evi-O for designing the very chic cover, and very chic pages, of this book. It was such an honour to have a person as brilliant as Evi involved in this project.

Thank you to Nas for being a constant sounding board for my ideas, and supporter of this book. Thank you to Ben and the whole Mob team. This book would not have happened without all I learnt with you, and all of your guidance.

To Mum and Dad, the original feeders of my insatiable appetite. I'm not sure another person on this earth has been born into a more loving environment. Anything that I am able to achieve is down to you making me feel like anything is possible. Thank you for all the dinners and endless encouragement. To my sisters – Ellie, Maddy, Phoebe and Mimi – my best cheerleaders. How lucky I am to have you as best friends and hype women, as well as the gorg models in this book. Thank you also to their better halves, The Wyburd Tarts – Olly, Luke, Maia and Harvey – and my baby niece Lyra. You lot are all magic. I'd also like to thank my Granny for lending her expert eye to proofreading for me, and my Grandma for all her encouragement.

I am lucky enough to not only have the bestest of family, but the greatest of friends. Thank you for all the evenings spent gossiping around a dinner table until the wee hours that have inspired this book. To Martha, Matty, Sarah and Nick; my school wimmxn and the BDH; to Hugh, Hannah Crosbie and to my beveraginos gang. I love you all immensely! Most of all, thank you to Kate, my original other half, who has been my rock for 26 years and counting. The runner of baths; sender of flowers; maker of thousands of cups of tea; co-host of countless boozy lunches. Truly the best friend a girl could wish for.

To Cam, my dream man. Not to mention the person who named this book! Thank you for enthusiastically giving feedback on every single recipe in this book, and your acceptance of your kitchen being turned upside down for several months. You have the patience of a saint, and your love and encouragement rocket fuels me. What a joy it is that I get to eat fish finger sandwiches on the sofa with you for the rest of my life.

About the author

Sophie Wyburd is a cook, recipe writer and presenter from South London. Sophie's varied career in food has seen her working as a restaurant chef, in food styling and heading up the food team at Mob. She now brings simple, comforting home cooking to the masses via social media and her newsletter, Feeder. You can also find her cooking up a storm at supper clubs all over London, and co-hosting *I'll Have What She's Having* and *A Bit of a Mouthful* podcasts.

3

Ebury Press, an imprint of Ebury Publishing
Penguin Random House UK
One Embassy Gardens, 8 Viaduct Gardens,
London. SW11 7BW

Ebury Press is part of the Penguin Random House group of companies
whose addresses can be found at global.penguinrandomhouse.com

Penguin
Random House
UK

First published by Ebury Press in 2024

www.penguin.co.uk

A CIP catalogue record for this book is available from the
British Library

ISBN 9781529909951

Design by Evi-O.Studio
Artworking by maru studio G.K.
Photography by Lizzie Mayson
Food styling by Esther Clark
Prop styling by Hannah Wilkinson

Colour origination by Altaimage Ltd
Printed and bound in Italy by L.E.G.O.

The authorised representative in the EEA is Penguin Random House
Ireland, Morrison Chambers, 32 Nassau Street, Dublin D02 YH68.

MIX
Paper | Supporting
responsible forestry
FSC
www.fsc.org   FSC® C018179

Penguin Random House is committed to a
sustainable future for our business, our readers
and our planet. This book is made from Forest
Stewardship Council® certified paper.